SMARTER BUSINESS STRONGER CA$HFLOW

HOW BUSINESS OWNERS CAN SMASH THEIR CASHFLOW CHALLENGES

PAUL ROACH

Disclaimer: The information in this book is of a general nature only and does not constitute Accounting, Business or Legal advice. It is not intended to replace the services of your Professional Advisors. Concerning the information contained in this book, readers should consult their own Accountant regarding their own individual business circumstances and needs.

You may wish to consult thecashflowcoach.global for specific advice to your business needs by contacting them directly at admin@thecashflowcoach.global.

The author, publisher and editor disclaim all responsibilities and liabilities to any person or business, arising directly or indirectly from either taking action or not taking action based on the information in this publication.

COPYRIGHT
© 2019 Paul Roach
All rights reserved. No portion of this book may be reproduced in any form without permission from the publisher, except as permitted by Australian copyright law. For permissions contact: admin@thecashflowcoach.global.

www.thecashflowcoach.global

Design for Success Pty Ltd ABN 75 622 800 560

ISBN: 978-0-6487202-0-1

Table of Contents

Introduction   1

Chapter 1
Warning: Being in business can kill you   7

Chapter 2
Sales: You can die with them, and definitely die without them   14

Chapter 3
When our labour is part of COGS   32

Chapter 4
Overheads   50

Chapter 5
It's a Balance Sheet for a reason   68

Chapter 6
Stock or not to stock?   81

Chapter 7
Look forward and know where you are going…   97

Chapter 8
Cash is king   109

Chapter 9
Extra essentials   128

Cashflow Sins Directory   135

Introduction
Smarter Business - The magic of making those damn Accounting Numbers work for YOU

My Perspective

Running a business is a bit like driving a car. Most of us tend to look forward and never take our eyes off the road in front. Others keep an eye on the rear vision mirror to check that the road behind us isn't littered with debris.

In my early working days as a Management Accountant, I seemed to spend a lot of time looking in the rear vision mirror and telling clients where they had been, occasionally picking up on some significant debris they had left on the road.

We knew what people were looking for out the front window, but as accountants are so often bogged down in processing information and completing reports, I never got the chance to get in early and head off problems or see how the reports could be used to make the business money.

Smarter Business Stronger Cashflow

This changed for me when I moved to a project role in a business that was losing a considerable amount of money and at real risk of being closed. I worked as part of a team that lead a $250M rebuild of the Mill Site and in doing so, turned the operating losses around. Every career move after that was to a smaller business in a broader role.

And Then....

A second turning point came when I took a consulting role.

The big get bigger and the small continue to struggle! Big Business makes it look easy. They seem to be able to change, evolve, right-size and capitalize on opportunities seamlessly. Having access to high level resources, the smartest and best people money can buy goes a fair way to simplifying how you can operate your business and how you can adequately research and resource expansion opportunities.

I started my career in this environment. I could easily see that access to skillsets and resources made this readily achievable. I must come clean and own up – I am a qualified accountant, CPA. I am also qualified in Supply Chain Management and Manufacturing. I spent years working with business owners using technology to streamline business processes and create a competitive advantage. My point of difference is that I now operate a Business Coaching business because even though I have held the CPA designation for thirty years or more I love

Introduction

supporting business owners to make more money... not just counting the money they've made.

Most 'normal' accountants are focused on statutory compliance and the issues this raises. They love to make sure your tax returns are done, sort through your BAS and take care of any other compliance related issues. They simply do not get time to really understand and review your business to know how you can make more on the bottom line.

This creates an issue because many business owners and entrepreneurs rely on their accountants to provide this service. If they have an accountant involved in their business, then they hope that in some way the accountant's input will increase certainty around the business's survival and profitability.

From what I have seen very few accountants give their clients practical ways of helping them to move forward and make more money. I believe that accountants have too much on their plate being in a compliance-driven world.

What is even worse is that accounting reports are hard-going, mysterious and do not really tell you the full story of what you need to know about your business.

Profit and Loss reports and Balance Sheets can be confusing, then there are Cashflows to contend with. Information is all over the place in different Accounting Reports. It's no wonder many business owners just give up trying to make sense of it all.

The Journey YOU are embarking on

This book takes you on a journey through your business from an entrepreneurial viewpoint. The aim of it is to give you some clear guidelines around what is important for you to know, what is important for you to implement, and how you manage the vital drivers of your business over time so your business can stay on track.

Your bottom-line profit is your story. You have control over this. I'm yet to see a business owner that would not like to increase their cashflow so they can pay their bills, buy good stuff and build up the money in their bank. Follow the guidelines, stay with it to the end of the book and that is what you will achieve.

Enjoy the journey. It will take you down pathways that that will develop skills you never knew about and that you didn't even know you needed. The faster you master this the earlier you will see results. As a business owner, a key part of your journey is learning how to smash your cashflow challenges!

Introduction

Smarter Business Stronger Cashflow

Empowering business owners to be able to make smarter decisions with better information is a key part of what I've been able to achieve. I have been fortunate enough to work with hundreds of businesses over the last thirty years; improving their structures and processes, working to take costs out of the business and helping them grow the top line that greatly impacts the bottom-line results.

What I have found is that this process is about digging deep and looking at numbers with a view to the **Third Dimension**. When I refer to numbers in 3D like this, I am talking about the Third Dimension being the ability to change the numbers over a period. This time period may be very short. The time frame may also be over a longer period depending on the urgency, the necessity for change and the complexity of what is involved.

Many of us will say our business is different and, in a way, we are unique. This book tends to focus on the key consistencies that I have found across all businesses.

This is the starting point, and this will get you to think about your business differently. If you take on board all of the information this book covers, you will make money from it. I guarantee that. I also acknowledge that some businesses will require additional work over and above what this book covers. Should this be the case, then get in touch with us.

This is a journey to get excited about! Every business owner dreams about making significantly more money on their bottom line – I'm going to show you how to do it. To give your business a healthier bottom-line and a much greater chance of longevity - full steam ahead and enjoy the journey!

Chapter 1
Warning: Being in Business can Kill YOU

My Journey... From the Office desk to The Emergency Room

"I'm sorry Mr. Roach, it's guilty until proven innocent in this environment...

"Hop in the wheelchair and we will take you straight to the Coronary Care Unit, and NO! You're not allowed to walk there."

As the male nurse pushed me along my mind was racing. I didn't feel that bad, I just felt like I had a heavy dose of hayfever combined with some shoulder and neck tightness - flu symptoms.

The pain had gone by now, I was just struggling a bit to breathe fully, with chest tightness and general unease. Lethargic.

The pathway from the doctor's surgery to the hospital was a little rough. We were going through the back entrance to the hospital. This had the look and feel of a basement entry, I remember it as a side entry to one of the loading docks thank goodness it was Saturday so there were no trucks backed in.

The faint smell of dampness, water stained carpet and the look of neglect was not the grand entry to hospital you see on TV, however the nurse who was pushing me had real urgency, like it was a life-and-death mission.

I was not in that zone, all I really wanted to do was rest, I was tired, not thinking clearly and not in a position to do much about anything that was happening.

I was reflecting how the last few years had been a rough road, tougher than life had thrown at me at any other point in my fifty odd years on this planet.

I honestly believed I had reached the bottom over the last few months and had made some good progress moving forward from that low point, but I was not ready for another setback in life.

Hadn't I had enough? Here I was again in the basement, both physically and emotionally.

In the gaps between the flurry of doctors, nurses and admin personnel I was alone with my own thoughts. Thoughts of how my dad had gone through a similar emergency trip to hospital a few years earlier but in a more significant way.

Chapter 1

Dad unfortunately didn't make it through his heart challenges. Our belief was that his death was caused by a medical error, an inadvertent over-sight or at best one of those extremely rare events happening. But what would happen to me?

My maternal grandfather died before I was born from a heart attack basically at the same age I was now. Would this be my final curtain call?

My mind was racing. Yes, my life insurance was paid up to date and in good shape. I knew I missed my parents; would my kids miss me? Hell yes. The thought of them not having me in their lives was devastating. The thought of missing out on my three daughters growing up caused my mind to race through the key events they had ahead of them that I should be a part of.

Loreta's mum had been on her own for over ten years and we'd seen the impact of that firsthand. Now for Loreta to potentially be on her own for thirty plus years - well, that did not sit well with me. I hadn't been able to convince Loreta that she would need a new partner if I dropped off the perch too early, I was not planning on testing it. We had been together a long time and planned to be together for at least that long again, it was time for the second half not the end of the game!

Then there was me; what had I not accomplished in this life that could now end prematurely? Truckloads was my thought, way too many things to even think about.

Bit by bit the results came back showing that I was one of the lucky ones!

What I gleaned from the nurses was astounding – I had a rare heart abnormality which meant that my heart was a different shape and the chambers and connections were different sizes, so the blood goes different directions compared to what happens in a normal heart.

Many people with these conditions often have fatal heart attacks in their 30s or 40s and nobody knows there was a problem until it's too late.

However, I had beaten the odds, I was alive, and I was eternally grateful.

The nights in hospital were rough... heart monitors are loud. Post-angiogram care is a half-hourly check of your groin!

Hospital beds are made for hospital efficiency, not patient comfort...

Being awake all night gave me time to think because as exhausted as my brain was, I really wanted to absorb these

Chapter 1

feelings to motivate me not to end up anywhere near a hospital for at least another twenty-five years.

Nothing personal, the staff were great, and I really like my heart specialist. He is calm, cool and collected – the perfect antidote to the fear and anxiety heart problems bring.

But now I knew how quickly things could end, I did not want to miss out on accomplishing everything I wanted to accomplish in this life. That would be tragic.

I vowed to "live while I'm alive... and sleep while I am dead" as the song goes.

WARNING: Being in Business can Kill YOU

My clients start working with me for countless different reasons. Much of the time it is through changing some of the variables we are focusing on through this book. Unfortunately, sometimes it is far more serious, and businesses need major surgery or in some rare occasions, it's time for the insolvency experts to step in. No matter where your business sits along that line of severity, there is real personal stress.

One of my clients simply refused to answer his mobile phone and spent his time away from work sitting at home with the curtains drawn and no lights on. Many clients simply do not sleep, or if they do sleep it's broken and limited. One was using prostitutes whilst many used alcohol as an escape. One headed towards dealing drugs and is a guest of Her Majesty's Prisons whilst many more are drug users. One client slept two hours a night. The result of all of this is many broken families and many business owners dealing with health issues.

I'd had my fair share of traumas in the years before my heart attack. Looking back, my Coach counted seven events that qualified over a four-year period leading up to it, from my dad's unexpected death to the last one was dealing with a crook in a business I had bought in to. Some of the traumatic events are now locked down in Confidentiality Agreements as a result of legal settlements I have received. No matter which way you look at it, that time period was the roughest of my life by a significant margin.

By the time I ended up in hospital, I had gone through severe anxiety and depression triggered by some of the early traumas and was finding my mojo was very low, causing a strain on my cashflow. From a practical point of view, I did exactly what I recommend in this book. **Remember that businesses are businesses, assets are assets, but your health is priceless.**

I knew I would be okay; I was one of the lucky ones who got the message. I took that learning on board so that I could help prevent catastrophic consequences for others and impart

Chapter 1

some of my knowledge to get smarter results across the business community.

I vowed to help business owners learn new skills they needed in mastering business, profitability and cashflow. This provided the inspiration for this book and would draw together the incredibly simple and powerful strategies I have gained in 30+ years working with in business.

Chapter 2
Sales - you can die with them, and definitely die without them

Sales are the lifeblood of every business. Plenty of sales, high margins and low overheads – perfect! What could and does go wrong?

Like blood flowing through your veins you can't live without them.

Sales/Margin Zone:

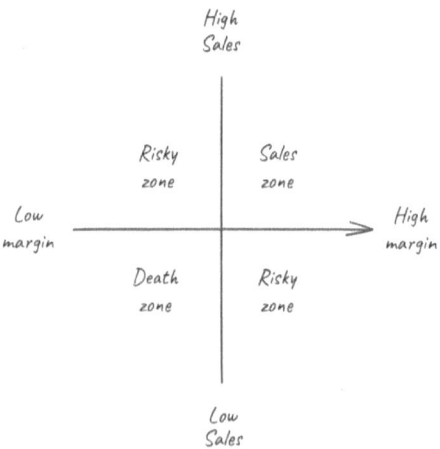

Chapter 2

Having a look at the graph, where does your business sit? Are you sitting in the Death Zone of low sales and low margin? Are you in one of the two Risky Zones where either Sales or Margin sit in the High Zone? Could your business die with high sales or live well with low sales? What are your risks and what needs to be mitigated?

Sales - The path to get in the 'Sales Zone'

The simple formula used to work out the sales figure on your Profit and Loss is:

The number of items you sell multiplied by the number of times you sell them multiplied by the price you sell at measured within a specific timeframe.

Number of items sold
X
Number of times sold
X
Individual sales price
=
Sales in the Profit & Loss

Straightforward, no tricks, no traps.

What you do not see in your Profit and Loss is the risks that are attached to that. Let's have a look at them.

It's time to dig deep and see what's not in the Financial statements and some seldom explored numbers which sit behind that sales figure.

The first thing I'm really curious about when I look at a business's Profit and Loss is the breakdown of the sales in terms of customers.

What I mean by this is measuring the value of what each customer brings to that sales figure on a monthly basis.

Simply by sorting the number and value of transactions by each of your customers from the largest down to the smallest you can see how much business each customer brings in for you.

When I meet business owners and salespeople, I challenge them to tell me their top ten customers and what percentage of business they're bringing in.

I'm yet to see or hear from one business owner that can get it in the right order and the right names on the page!

I'm not sure why this is, but I suspect it's the thrill of the next sale and the next customer rather than focusing on the existing loyal customer base.

Chapter 2

Concentration Risk

I started working with this business owner - let's call him Peter.

As part of the initial review, we had a look at these numbers in his sales figures and found that 90% of his business over the previous 5 years had effectively come from one customer.

Peter had a good steady business with several employees and had been able to earn a fairly good living from this. We both acknowledged that his income was not as good as it could have been as there were number of other issues in the business. (We will talk more about those issues as we continue to go through the book because it is a classic case study.)

The unfortunate part for Peter was that he had 90% of business coming from one customer who without warning decided to source most of its product range offshore!

This customer was going to keep a small number of ad hoc products in the local market that had shorter lead times but nothing like what Peter needed to stay viable.

For Peter this meant he had effectively 2 months to bolster his business as he was going to lose approximately 90% of sales income from this customer.

The Human Impact on Business

How do you think Peter felt now?

He was totally stressed, worrying he would lose everything he had built up – even his home which had secured a business loan. He was well beyond his ability to cope by the time we met – which, unfortunately for Peter, four months after the customer had taken business offshore.

Peter's business was suffering from what we call **Concentration Risk;** putting too many eggs in one basket and relying on that one source of business to keep the blood flowing in the veins of the business.

It was unfortunate for Peter because he had a long-standing relationship with this customer, the quality of his workmanship was excellent, and the pricing structure was fair to both sides.

However, most businesses are under competitive pressure to be able to find a solution to their problem and reduce their cost structure.

Here in Australia, a lot of manufacturing goes offshore, and I think it's a global phenomenon that the world is now a single marketplace to a fairly large extent.

Chapter 2

We can control what we can control but outside of that we have no control.

It was a long slow journey moving forward as Peter had no marketing in place, had rusty sales skills and no cash reserves.

Peter did however have great energy and a will to move forward quickly.

We tightened the cost structure and went full on with sales and marketing. A new style of business and a really demanding time for the owner!

Like most of us, Peter had a partner and dependent children, and the stress of overhauling his business naturally impacted his family. But his family bonded together and worked through this tough time.

How would your business survive if it lost a major customer or 90% of the work from your biggest customer? Would you survive or would your business end?

What's the learning?

Cashflow Sin #1

Putting all your eggs in one basket can be a major problem for your business.

DOLLARS & SENSE EXERCISE #1

Have a look at your sales mix by customer and by product and see if your concentration levels from that one customer or reliance on that one product range is too high.

How do you know if it's too high?

Simply, if you lost that customer or you lost that product your business would struggle to survive or suffer a significant set-back.

Want to avoid the pitfalls of Peter's business and looking for consistently stronger cashflow? Go ahead, review where you are at, if needed put a plan in place to fix it and GIFS! (Get it &%#$ing sorted!)

For free stuff, useful tips and course work, head to our website: www.thecashflowcoach.global

Chapter 2

Time Warp Risk

I was working with a franchise a few years ago that had been running for almost ten years. This business had never increased the sell price of its core product range which accounted for around 75% of their sales. In other words, the franchisor did not allow its franchisees to exceed its current maximum retail price for the core range. This pricing had been held constant for just under ten years and it was easy to see from the Franchise Benchmark Standards that margins were getting severely squished.

The franchisor was claiming that tightening market conditions meant they needed to keep the price down to attract new customers to business. There was some sad, misguided belief that this would help keep the pressure on the competition. It took a bit of pushing and shoving but within a few months the franchisor had agreed to do a market review of pricing and we saw the first price rise come through in a 10-year period. Not surprisingly there was plenty of opportunity to increase pricing on the core range of products sold.

The pleasing thing about this was that the price increase had virtually no impact on the number of customers that the business serviced.

This outcome totally contradicted what the franchisor had been saying, that they needed to keep prices low to keep the customers.

The reality of the situation was the customers were accepting of price rises as a natural part of doing business. Not wanting to stop there, we continued to push the Franchisor to implement a strategy of putting in a regular price rise through or at least a market review, every six months. This saw a consistent increase in prices that allowed the business to breathe.

Time Warp Risk

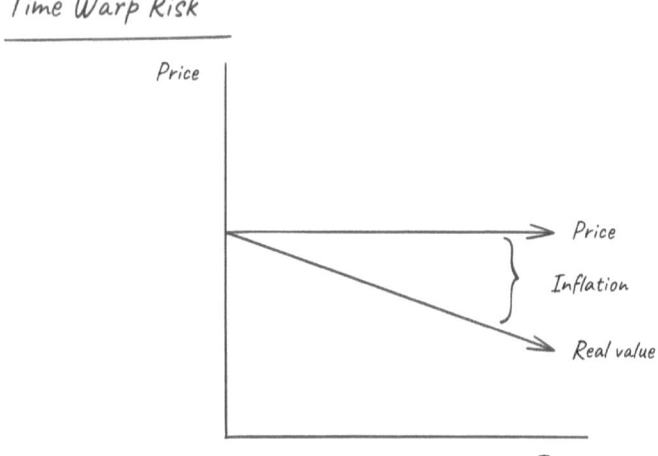

Chapter 2

Cashflow Sin #2

Reviewing and updating pricing regularly is part of your job, either do it or manage it or shoot yourself in the foot through leaving money on the table!

Dollars & SENSE EXERCISE #2

Want to avoid the pitfalls of what hundreds of these franchisees went through for an extended period? Looking to achieve consistently stronger cashflow? Go ahead, review where you are at, review the pricing in the marketplace and, if needed put a plan in place to fix it and GIFS!

> For free stuff, useful tips and course work, head to our website: www.thecashflowcoach.global

Step 2: Reclaim

The next part of the process with the franchise was to try and catch up some of the lost ground from the previous ten years or so.

We pushed the franchisor hard and they finally agreed to undergo a cost review of things that were in their control, i.e.

core products in their list of Cost of Goods Sold (COGS). We did see at this point a growth in sales coupled with a small decrease in the COGS measured as a percentage of sales adding up to an overall increase in profit.

The most important thing achieved at this point was the increase in the selling price of the individual products leading to an increase in the overall revenue of the business. There was a small decline in customer numbers in light of the price rises, but revenue increased comfortably above any losses. We also found that those losses were only loss of customers temporary. We found that customers overcame the initial shock of a price rise and came back to the business.

What is also important here is that I've seen many businesses continue to discount their products and services heavily to attract business. Whilst this might seem a good idea of the time, it is a very fast way to kill your business. In fact, it is a cashflow sin to discount your products or services beyond the level where it makes your business viability unsustainable.

What is interesting about the way most accounting systems work is that we don't see the level of discount that gets carried with products. What happens is that the net sales value after the discount has been applied is what gets recorded in the sales ledger. So, we don't actually see how much we are giving away at any point in time unless we look deep into the figures behind the sales figure in our accounting system.

Chapter 2

Cashflow Sin #3

Not focusing on your Cost of Goods Sold (COGS) will squeeze your Gross Margin and reduce your cashflow. Regularly reviewing your COGS is an important part of owning your business.

Dollars & SENSE EXERCISE #3

It's time to review your COGS – Get to IT and see what you can save and add to your cashflow! Review where you are at, review the cost pricing in the marketplace and, if needed, put a plan in place to fix it and GIFS!

> For free stuff, useful tips and course work, head to our website: www.thecashflowcoach.global

Disasters through Discounting

I am yet to see a business that does not discount in one-way shape or form. As much as we educate not to discount, maybe the reality is a question of controlling the amount of discounting that occurs. Simply, some customers receive discounts for certain reasons, the discounts get applied and remain in place, seemingly permanently.

When was the last time you reviewed the rules around the discounts you give? Are they still valid? Are we able to limit the discounting which effectively increases our prices?

It is time to look at the Gross Margin we receive on each of our customers. Then look at what proportion of sales account for, at what margin, and ask ourselves the question: what are we giving away? Are we able to scale this back a bit to bolster our top and bottom lines? Maybe a better question is: how do we scale back our discounting?

Cashflow Sin #4

Discounting reduces our Gross Margin and is often disastrous financially for our business.

Dollars & SENSE EXERCISE #4

If you want to change profitability quickly and know it is one thing that really needs to be reduced, preferably eliminated – pull back on discounting. Go ahead, review where you are at with each customer, review the discounting you are giving and, if needed, put a plan in place to fix it and GIFS!

For free stuff, useful tips and course work, head to our website: www.thecashflowcoach.global

Chapter 2

Being a Banker in your Business

Money in the bank! Well, if we've sold something, we might have an expectation that we're going to be paid. What could possibly go wrong? We do the work; we sell the products and a customer takes receipt. Why would we not get paid?

There's a whole stack of reasons why we may not get paid.

Firstly, let's just get really clear in our minds that the sale is not complete until the money is in the bank. Secondly, let's accept the fact that many things can go wrong. Your customers may find reasons why they don't want to pay you. They might look for defects and might start to question the price. All sorts of things. Your customers may also experience cashflow challenges from their own business, and they may have people not paying them, so the cash is in short supply. You may also find that some businesses go bankrupt and then you have very little chance of getting paid at all. We will cover off debt later in the book, however, getting paid for what you sell on credit is not always easy.

It's important that we take action to protect ourselves and our businesses against the situations that may arise from us not getting paid. It would be great if we could always get paid on delivery or even before delivery. With credit cards and COD some types of industries are suited to this and you get paid.

Smarter Business Stronger Cashflow

As soon as things go on an account, we've got an element of trust. Sometimes they're in our control, sometimes our trust is well-founded, but sometimes it's misplaced.

Profit and Loss may not be Cash in the Bank

When understanding a Profit and Loss Statement and other financial statements, it is important we understand whether we are recognising sales that have been paid on a cash basis or sales that have accrued in the accounting system whether it is paid or unpaid.

The difference between the two is simple. If we go on a cash basis, we only recognise it when it's been paid. If we go on an accrual basis then we recognise the sale whether it's paid or remains unpaid. We can do the same with our GST for the ATO and there is no obligation for us to keep the two the same. We can run an accrual basis for reporting and a cash basis for the ATO. The advantage of this is that we are not reliant on receiving or paying money before the ATO gets paid. This means that if something does go wrong, we're not prepaying ahead of the curve or just receiving money on the way through.

What is important in our understanding here is to acknowledge the fact that cash can be different to what's in a profit and loss.

Chapter 2

Cashflow Sin #5

Extending credit terms to our customers strains our cashflow AND we increase our risks of not being paid.

Dollars & SENSE EXERCISE #5

In many businesses I work with, this is the first place to look to change their cash situation. It is the role of the business owner to collect from debtors, reduce the amounts outstanding and eliminate credit terms. Ensure this is done and maintained – this is your business's money you have loaned to someone else! GIFS!

Digging deep exercise #5A

Here is an added Digging Deep Exercise around this. Look at all the money that actually did come in during the time period in question (the actual cash receipts) and have a look at how much money actually went out (cash payments). Then see which way that sits. Have you received more than you're paying, or have you paid more than what you have received?

Getting your head around this is a big step in understanding how we can move forward and better understand the position of your business.

For free stuff, useful tips and course work, head to our website: www.thecashflowcoach.global

Chapter 2

Some Technical Accounting 'stuff'

If your business is registered for GST (Goods and Services Tax) - which is the underlying assumption for this book - GST is excluded from Profit and Loss Reports.

Why? GST you collect is a Liability payable to the ATO and GST you pay as part of your purchases is like an Asset and can be refunded from the ATO or used to reduce the GST Liability. The GST is never yours really as most businesses will pay the ATO more than they receive.

How Do you Do?

From how you rated your business at the top of this chapter to where your thoughts are now, what needs to change and how quickly does it need to change? How do you move out of the Death Zone or from a Risky Zone into the Sales and Margin Zone? We had a quick look at what sits behind our Profit and Loss in the details of Customer Volumes and Margins. We also jumped to our Balance Sheet and the details of our Debtors and developed a cashflow review of actual cash in and cash out. This emphasises that as business owners we need to look in several places to understand what our financials are telling us. This also helps us know what drivers we need to focus on to get the best cashflow results from our business.

Chapter 3
When our Labour is part of COGS

Almost every business owner I have worked with is concerned about the prospect of raising their prices and resists this. All have been frustrated with their margins on chargeable labour, however almost none of them have really understood the true cost of each employee that generates income for their business.

Let's get a better understanding of revenue and costs here, along with some key strategies to maximise our top line.

Remember back in the previous chapter I spoke of Peter and his business challenges around Concentration Risk. In this chapter, we're going to look at how we got his business profitable quickly.

The strategy we undertook worked, and Peter was making his best profits ever as a business owner. Why he had not made good profits previously was largely because he had not learned what is contained in this chapter. For a metal fabrication business there was very poor control of costs on the shop floor. Peter was an expert tradesman, not an educated business owner. We will continue Peter's story later.

What does it really cost us to sell what we do?

We are in business to sell either goods or services or both. Let's have a look at what the Cost of Goods (COGS) are. No tricks or surprises, it's straightforward with goods we sell: we buy something, and then sell it at a higher price than what we bought it for. Services on the other hand, particularly if we are providing those services from internal staff members, is often a little more complicated and a little more difficult to keep track of. Whilst legal and accounting firms have this licked, I am not so sure tradies and the like have it fully under control.

There are some things that I believe are just non- negotiable, and we have hit one just here. People in a business are either:

1. Revenue Generating (Chargeable Resources) – these would include electricians and plumbers in a trade business, salespeople and people on the factory floor making and fabricating things to sell.
2. Non-Revenue Generating (Non-Chargeable) – Accounts, HR, Marketing
3. A combination of the above – often technical people who do a combination of chargeable repair work and some non-chargeable warranty work.

Why do we need to get to this level of detail? Simply put, it's smarter business and makes our job of managing our businesses simpler and easier. Here is why!

Getting to the Detail to get Smarter

Let's look at a simple plumbing business. We have plumbers, we have apprentices, and we probably have some hired help as well. This is in addition to the business owner and possibly someone in the office. For the purposes of this exercise I'm the owner and the person in the office so not directly on the tools and not chargeable. All the other members of the team are a chargeable resource and generate revenue for the business.

I argue that COGS should include all the cost of keeping these people on payroll which includes what they're paid and the employment on-costs that need to be accrued to cover their costs. This includes items such as Annual Leave, Sick Leave, Public Holiday Pay, Superannuation, Workers Compensation Insurance and anything else that falls in that category. Along with the direct costs of keeping them there such as cars, uniforms, phones and share of office space.

Like cans of baked beans on the supermarket shelf – they are there to be sold every day – 480 minutes of solid goodness.

Chapter 3

C.O.G.S Labour

What does it really cost to do what we do?

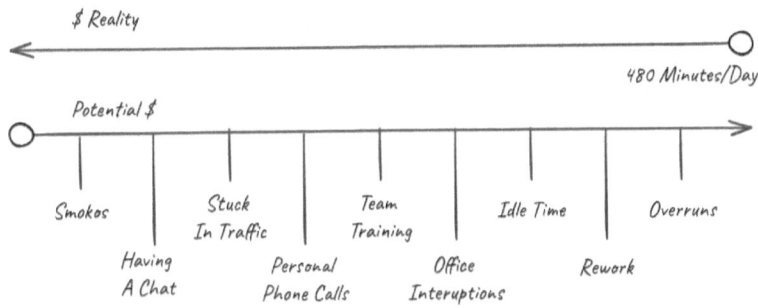

For the sake of simplicity let's assume that employees are working a 40-hour week. There are different parts to this equation, firstly if we are paying them for 40 hours a week, how many hours are they charging to jobs? In other words, what is the level of productivity that they actually charge to the customer.

For some business owners this may seem like a very silly question. Normally, the answer is to charge as much of their time to the customer as they can. I have seen chargeability in trades industries as low as 15 hours a week for a 40-hour week worked. I hear from the guys that they're very busy; I hear from the owner that they're very busy – but interestingly, I can always see that the numbers tell the real story. If the business is busy and the plumbers have work, why are they not charging 40 hours a week for 40 hours worked?

This is the interesting part - there's lots and lots of reasons why this might be happening, but chances are, there are a few major ones. Let's have a look at them.

How to get your Team to be more Productive

Firstly, I think that as people, we like to have work in front of us. When we know that we have another job to go to, it is often the thing that keeps us moving and keeps us motivated. Good scheduling means keeping work in front of people. I'm not saying you should push your staff beyond what's reasonable, just to keep new work as a top priority.

Secondly, there is a great deal of merit in being organised. Being able to get to a job quickly, get underway as soon as you get there, and having what you need when you need it, really helps with your productivity. Being organised for the next day when you finish the day before means you can hit the ground running and not waste or lose time before you start.

In one of the plumbing businesses I was coaching, we found that some of the guys were losing up to two hours at the start of each day just getting organised. This was not their fault, as the owner of the business asked them to come in for a meeting every day to give them their job sheets and organise what they needed to do. It's great to have that face-to-face

Chapter 3

contact however, these guys were spending over an hour on the road each way getting from one location to the next - just to have a chat with the boss and get some paperwork every morning. We quickly set up a computer and a printer at the home of the plumber that was the furthest away from the office. Now it was really easy to email things through, print off job sheets and any other paperwork that was needed, and suddenly we found that plumber and his apprentice were able to bill an additional ten hours a week to clients.

Keep hold of the umbilical cord

It is essential to maintain contact with people who operate remotely from the business. In this instance, the owner organised a separate catch up with each team member during the week, in addition to a weekly get together with all the team to keep up that interaction. Within just a three-weeks, we saw a massive change from 15 chargeable hours (in a 40 hour week) when we started to 25 chargeable hours per week. It took a little bit longer to get to 30 chargeable hours a week, but certainly within two months we had found that the labour chargeability had doubled from the original starting point.

To get from 30 to 35 - which was the next target - required a mindset shift. The change required was in the self-belief that this could be done. We are not here to treat our employees as slaves; however, to be less than 90% chargeable in a 40-

hour week from a chargeable resource when the work is available is a bit of a problem!

It took a little while to build the business's marketing up to be able to generate the additional work to keep all the plumbers on board. Because the chargeability had doubled, they were now getting through twice as much work in a week. It was interesting how much work they were missing previously because they believed they were too busy charging 15 hours a week.

Within three months, we were pushing over 30 hours a week on average for each employee. Things seem to level out a bit at around 35 hours a week. We found that that was the new equilibrium point where employees were comfortable with their workload, and there was time to do the things like restocking the van, training, and spending some time quality time with their fellow employees and the owners of the business. Not a bad result - in fact, I would call it an excellent result!

Unlike the cans of baked beans on the supermarket shelf, selling labour has a unique time value. If you miss it, it is gone, and you cannot get it back again. Be ready to capitalise on the 480 minutes available to you each and every workday!

Chapter 3

Cashflow Sin #6

Paying a workforce and NOT maximising their potential for the time they are at work fails to maximise cashflow opportunity and may in fact put a strain on your cashflow if their workflow is not cashflow positive.

Dollars & SENSE EXERCISE #6

In many businesses I work with, maximising chargeability is one of the top five areas I look to change their cash situation. You do not get a free can of baked beans at the supermarket, you need to pay for each one you purchase. The same applies to employees, unless there is a reason for them not to be chargeable for a specific time, focus on generating revenue through them for 100% of their work week - get to it! Your business's money is paying their wages, you have missed an opportunity! GIFS!

Digging deep exercise #6A

Here is an added Digging Deep exercise around this. Consider the reasons why your chargeable employees are not 100% chargeable. If you are not satisfied with these reasons, then how will you prevent this in the future? How are you, and your business, learning from this to operate a smarter business and stronger cashflow?

For free stuff, useful tips and course work, head to our website: www.thecashflowcoach.global

My Experience

When I was consulting some years ago, I looked back at the chargeable hours I was working. Clients often had control over the time I was on site and given all circumstances this is what I achieved: across a three-year period, I was averaging 1,650 hours invoiced per year. That was about a 37.5 hours per week for every week worked. The model we had in place was four days Monday to Thursday and a half day on Friday with time in the office generally non-chargeable on Friday afternoons.

Chapter 3

I was comfortable with this arrangement. I found that if I pushed myself beyond this, I would start to get worn out and tired but if I slipped too much under this level, I got frustrated that I wasn't busy enough and possibly not learning enough. Everyone has their own equilibrium.

As business owners, it's up to us to determine the workload of our employees. Our employees don't determine their workload. Having said that, I accept that everybody's productivity will be different and certain employees will be better suited to specific roles or styles of work.

Now let's start getting Serious!

Employees:

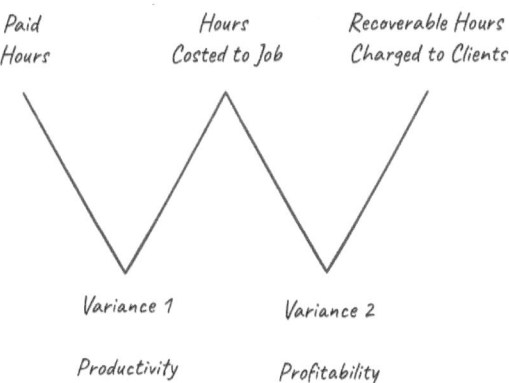

The second aspect of labour to consider when it's part of your Cost of Goods is how much of the time that you're charging to jobs is included in the budget or is recoverable on the job.

Let's simplify this a bit. Let's assume that we have quoted ten hours for the job to be done, whatever that job maybe. We get Fred to work on the job. Unfortunately, Fred is having a bad day and makes a few mistakes. Fred gets the job done in fifteen hours. We find we are not able to recover the additional time from the customer as Fred got it wrong.

However, if Fred took fifteen hours to perform quoted work of ten hours and the error was in the quoting and we still couldn't recover it, then the person who did the quote needs to learn from this. We can't crucify the employee for all the variances that occur.

Tracking the reasons for variances helps better define the area of our business that might need improvement. Building this internal knowledge base is fundamental to our business moving forward.

Chapter 3

Cashflow Sin #7

Work and product defects come straight off the bottom line and represent a lost opportunity. Eliminating these is a top priority.

Dollars & SENSE EXERCISE #7

Monetise the value of defects and the lost opportunity to give yourself the reality check of what is happening in your business – get to it! It is your business's money; you have missed an opportunity! GIFS!

For free stuff, useful tips and course work, head to our website: www.thecashflowcoach.global

---

Parkinson was Psychic

I am a firm believer in Parkinson's Law. The theory behind Parkinson's Law is that the work you are doing will fit into the time that you have allocated to it. The work we do will fill the available time. Applying this to when we are allocating work to employees in a business goes like this: if we allocate two hours to do the work, it will more than likely take them just over two hours. If allocate two and a half hours, it will probably take closer to two and a half hours to do the work - irrespective of the fact that we could do it in two. Why is this the case? Well simply put, human nature says that when we're under a timeline constraint, in any given hour we get more done in the last minute than the previous 59. It's easy to fall behind when we think we have time ahead of us to do things. My experience tells me that keeping work lined up for people and limiting the time they can spend on it greatly increases the productivity of the workforce.

Cashflow Sin #8

Letting your focus drift away from chargeability and profitability can become a habit, stay focused on this as it becomes a key element of stronger cashflow.

Dollars & SENSE EXERCISE #8

There will always be a range in quality and speed on work performed, rank your team in each of these two areas and set training targets for them moving forward – get to it! It is your business's money; you have missed an opportunity! GIFS!

For free stuff, useful tips and course work, head to our website: www.thecashflowcoach.global

Chapter 3

Closing the Loop

I have always seen value in closing the loop with information fed back to employees. For example, I feel there is value in providing employees with a report on chargeable hours against a chargeable budget for the time worked back on a weekly basis. Employees don't have control over what hourly rate they are charged out at, that's a decision for the business owner to be making.

Employees also cannot charge when they do not have chargeable work to do or they're asked to do non-chargeable work. This is the point I was making above. I do feel however that if they have a budget to reach that they can take ownership of, then giving them feedback on how they are tracking is valuable. It is important that employees have feedback to ascertain if they are under, equal to, or over their budget on a weekly basis.

In addition to the above, I also see value in being able to provide information to specific or the whole of the business, to appropriate employees on a weekly basis. I mentioned above that accounting and legal firms have mastered this. Human nature says nobody wants to be towards the bottom of the list. Nobody wants to underperform. Providing feedback is a matter of encouraging the business and its staff to perform at a certain level.

Keep the Chargeable Resources Chargeable

I am a keen supporter of businesses that keep their chargeable resources chargeable and move their non-chargeable resources into chargeable roles as required. It is a mindset shift. For someone that is used to being chargeable, keep them chargeable. This keeps them in their existing mindset.

To move a non-chargeable resource, such as an admin person, into a chargeable role requires a mindset shift that is often difficult and transition back the other way. Your business will benefit by keeping people focused on the tracks that they are on. Just try to make sure that they are measured accordingly to the chargeable and non-chargeable nature. As a rule of thumb, I suggest disclosing enough information to encourage employees; however, not so much that you breach confidentiality within your business.

Benchmarks

I'm constantly asked by business owners what their gross profit should be. Normally they see this as a percentage. Should my gross profit be 40%, should it be 80%, or should it be 4%? The reality is that every industry is different. I have seen businesses that operate within 80% gross profit margin and struggle to make money. I have also seen businesses

Chapter 3

where the industry average is between 2 and 4% gross profit and make good money.

The concept of benchmarking your business to see its performance against others in your industry is one that is new to most business owners. The Australian Taxation Office publishes benchmarks across different Industries. While these may be broad; it does give you a good indicator as to where you are sitting. The Tax Office also uses this information to find people outside the benchmarks. This information can then be used as grounds to possibly audit a business. This could be a bit unfortunate for some business owners however, if you're not within the benchmarks, what needs to change for you to get back there?

This Week	This Month	Year to Date
Fred	George	Bruce
Harry	Andy	Fred
George	Fred	Pete
Pete	Harry	Andy
Andy	Pete	Anthony

Smarter Business Stronger Cashflow

Cashflow Sin #9

Work with the mindset of employees and human nature. To make it easy to stay focused, most of us want to be towards the top of the Leader Board. Not having a little competition can adversely impact cashflow.

Dollars & SENSE EXERCISE #9

How do you rate with the above? Are within the benchmarks? Are you a leader within or above the benchmarks? Not sure? Get to it! It is your business's money; you have missed an opportunity! GIFS!

For free stuff, useful tips and course work, head to our website: www.thecashflowcoach.global

How Do You Do?

Chargeable Labour Slide Rate

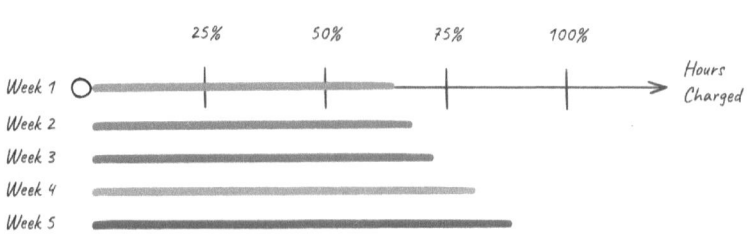

Chapter 3

Kaizen is a Japanese word for continuous improvement where these changes have a significant impact over time. If you are not getting solid performances with your direct labour, then change the fundamentals quickly and focus on Kaizen for the remainder. Your frustration is indirectly proportional to your cashflow. Neither frustration nor under-performing cashflow is good for you or your business. All the variables discussed become a key part of the profit of your business and directly impact your cashflow.

Think about Peter from my example earlier in the book. For Peter, *kaizen* meant cash in the bank for the first time – ever. His stress diminished and his business was running better than it had ever done. His business was tight, his team was onboard with the new regime, and product quality was exceptional. It was a sensational turnaround – however, it was still not enough, as we will discover later.

Chapter 4
Overheads

So far, we have been on a journey looking at our Sales and how we can convert them to cash more quickly. We looked at how our COGS impacts our Gross Profit and saw how we can maximise opportunity here. The risk here is that the Gross Profit gets eaten up in overheads and you, as the owner, then gets nothing!

I regularly see both sides of the coin, the first where the overhead cost of the business is disproportionate to the rest of the business. The other side is where the overhead is run too tightly and the business struggles to breathe.

We hit capacity with a fabrication business I was doing some work previously. The business grew to a point where the existing overhead structure just could not take on any further growth. After some investigation we discovered a new quoting software product that had recently been released that was specific to their industry. This was able to reduce the time spent on quoting, job management, time-sheeting and payroll. Simply put, the business was then able to grow an additional 30% with the same overhead.

Chapter 4

Keeping it Lean

What we are looking for is just like a good bit of steak, all meat and no fat. We want to keep overhead costs tight, but not stupidly so. I sometimes think that when businesses start to make money, the mindset changes - that there is suddenly room in the business to start being silly around overheads.

Lean is a concept developed in manufacturing businesses meaning the elimination of waste. Waste covers a multitude of sins from idle time on the shop floor, through to overstocking of inventory and any defects requiring rework. Lean is also about not running at optimum and wasting effort.

I'm not saying you should be stupid about overheads. However, there is a fine balance between necessities and luxuries. I feel there is also a fine balance between the level of overhead you need to keep the business operational and have some capacity for growth versus running them too tight and being silly. Here is one example where overheads severely strained the operating cashflow of a business.

Cut the fat before it clogs the Heart

I've seen a family business that is turning over around $8M and has an investment of roughly $1M worth of luxury cars sitting in the car park and family members' houses. The business may have at one point been able to afford this, however certainly not when time went on! As the business went into tougher times, the owner chose to continue to maintain the high standard of cars at the same level for his family members that were employed in the business and even some that were not; crazy!

Get the Blood to Flow

Another extreme I have seen is business owners working sixteen hours a day, six days a week. This has been the case even when the business has been making good profits and easily able to afford to employ additional team members. This has been a lifestyle choice by the owners, not a peak in demand in the business cycle. How fast can this strategy kill your business? Pretty well two birds with one bullet, your business first then you.

However, scaring you is not my primary motive here. My motive here is to help you understand a slightly different perspective on how overheads can work. I feel that many business owners become isolated in their business and don't necessarily see the opportunities that can lie outside their four walls; so, let's head on into this journey.

Performance Standards

If your employees don't know what they are meant to be doing, then how do they know what to do? Seems a very simple question however, very few businesses that I have worked with have documented what employees need to do. Sure, most know on a day-to-day basis what their primary function is, however the timeliness and responsiveness of what they do, can be somewhat questionable. Simple key performance indicators (KPIs) and a measurement of those over time will change their focus quickly. This will help drive the service standards in your business and help you identify any potential gaps.

Practical $ and Sense

In the first part of this book, we identified Sales and COGS. After we get our Gross Profit figure, we then need to deduct our overhead costs to come up with a Net Profit.

We need to ask very simple questions like, "if I'm charging labour by the hour, how many hours do I need to charge before I have recouped my overheads and hit a breakeven point?"

It does seem a little strange to me that business owners don't understand how many hours per day or per week their business needs to charge or how many products they need to move so they can cover their overheads. At the end of the day it is only after all of these costs have been paid that we can pull out some profits.

So essentially, what is your sales level per day or week or month? How many hours do you need to charge? What products do you need to sell? What's your factory production level required so you can achieve a break even? Simple, practical dollars and sense: we should know our break-even point.

Cashflow Sin #10

Go through your profit and loss. Calculate the numbers. I prefer you do it by hand because then we get a real cognitive learning experience and work out exactly where your break-even point is. Use that as a tool to drive you to a minimum daily activity level. Go and do it, now is the time!

Chapter 4

Dollars & SENSE EXERCISE #10

Is your business running too tight, too slow and potentially missing opportunities? Alternatively, is it running too fat and lazy and of risk of premature death from Overhead Obesity? Cast a fresh set of eyes over it from a distance. Ask yourself "what if..." for each scenario. Literally go and sit on the beach and think hard on this. GIFS!

For free stuff, useful tips and course work, head to our website: www.thecashflowcoach.global

---

Smart(er)

The isolation of having your own business can be significantly detrimental when it comes to moving your business forward with smarter business practices and technology. Let me give you an example.

One of my clients' employees had been with the same business for fifteen years and had seen multiple business owners in that time. Technology had moved on, and many years before she had been required to take charge of it. A simple enhancement like connecting automated bank feeds into the accounting systems was a major point of resistance.

For the size of the business and the number of transactions, having automated bank feeds would have saved approximately five hours per week in work time. Five hours per week, across a full year, is a significant cost for that business to wear. It's not just the cost of the additional money; it's the opportunity cost of what was missed by what other savings could have been implemented with this as well. In fact, I believe this employee was paid overtime to operate inefficiently!

It is the parts of the role that add value that should be rewarded; look for ways to have single entry for all information and avoiding multiple entry and multiple systems; use Customer Relationship Management (CRMs) to track activities with your future customer funnel all make for the opportunity for better decision making.

Business-to-Business (B2B) accounting transactions have been around for years now. QR and barcodes for many years more. Investment value was always an issue previously, now not so much. Re-assess this if you can see an upside.

When needed, payroll software that interfaces to time tracking clock-in and clock-out tools are now commonplace with a relatively low investment level. Working smarter will help drive a lower cost base for you to run your business from.

These are just some of the low hanging fruit before we even get serious about the new levels IT reaches every year. We want machines and automation, not increased labour and wages costs.

For most business owners, this is a daunting task and probably out of reach. Out of reach because we are busy getting through each day. The ability to focus on working smarter across our business in addition to our current workloads often feels like heading into fantasy land!

I have found that once we put some structure around our thoughts, things get easier and results get magnified. A bit like eating the elephant one bite at a time. Start very small: what can I do differently than could possible save me thirty minutes in a day? Implement it. Then use that time saving to focus your creative thoughts and energy to move to the next potential saving.

It may work best for you to focus on this daily for a short period, or every few days for a longer period, or maybe a weekly commitment works for you. There is a time to get your team involved, focused and motivated.

O-A-O-D-D

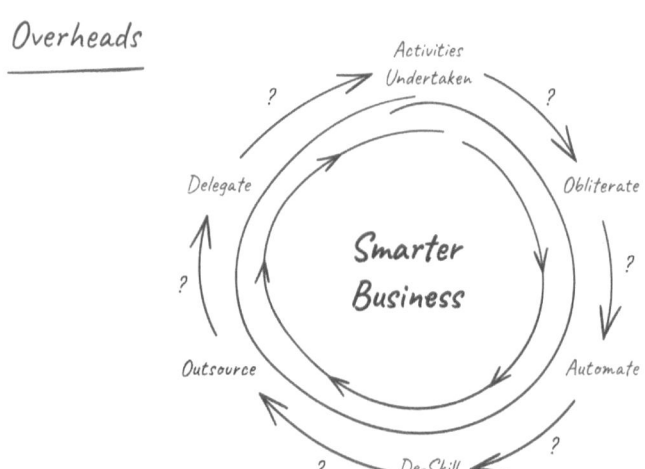

Every dollar you save in overhead goes directly into your Net Profit. Every bit of time we free up for ourselves through getting our business to work smarter gives us the opportunity to go for growth or take some time out and value our lives outside of work. Applying this process has given many business owners a much-needed boost to profitability and a much-needed reduction in their workload.

Let's get real about this and let's get savage. How do we cut or keep our operating costs at a minimum? We are in business to make money. Let's get on with the job.

Chapter 4

The acronym O-A-D-O-D simply stands for:
- **O**bliterate
- **A**utomate
- **D**e-Skill
- **O**utsource
- **D**elegate

It is a simple cycle through each one of these activities.

The functions that get done, do we still need to do them, or can we **obliterate** them?

If we can't obliterate them can we **automate** them?

If we can't automate them are, we able to **de-skill** the tasks or some of the tasks?

If we look at **outsourcing** or keeping them in house can we de-skill the process in any way shape or form?

If we cannot de-skill, then can we **delegate**?

If we can de-skill, can we still **delegate**?

When I'm talking about this process, I'm not generally talking about an entire job. I'm talking about functions within a job. I don't know how many times I have come across situations with there are senior people paid big salaries and a significant

59

portion of their time is spent doing menial tasks. Yet in the same business the people most capable of performing the menial tasks are sitting there with nothing to do.

The situation above with the bank feeds was very simply resolved. It was a simple exercise of training that person in setting up and running bank feeds on the system which was a very simple thing to do. Then it was just a requirement that that this had to be done moving forward. It was then that person had extra time and extra capacity to be able to do other things. We moved some other functions from someone else across to that person which meant one person in this organisation was able to get on the road and see potential new customers one day a week. This move generated real results for the business as that person won a couple of good customers over in a very short period.

Sometimes it is putting all the key people in the one office that makes a difference. This was particularly evident in one business I was working with where the Production Office and Accounts Teams were in separate offices in separate buildings literally ten metres apart. The amount of time spent phoning each other or walking between offices with queries was ridiculous. This was systematic of other issues within the business; however, these would take some time to work through. The quick fix to improve productivity and lower employee stress levels was to literally knock a wall down and create space in one building and relocate all employees to one central office. This happened at a time when one employee had just resigned and was working through their Notice Period; they were not replaced. The other employees easily coped with the increased workload as a result of their newfound ease of communicating.

Some Practical Examples to get us Thinking

Obliterate - We have all seen the massive impact technology has made on our lives. Phone systems have come a long way in recent years. The much-prized receptionist position has disappeared in many businesses replaced with automated phone systems or a handset at reception when you walk through the door. The Receptionist would often take the cash and cheques to the bank and the mail to the post office - I would put money on these tasks being eliminated in many businesses at least four days a week, if not entirely!

Automate – when things just happen! Simple automated reminders as text messages, emails or calendar appointments help take costs out of a business and increase the probability of clients attending their appointments, collecting their purchases or moving their car when its fully charged.

De-Skill – Accountants seem to have this one under control. The basics get done by the graduates, then reviewed by the managers before a further review and sign-off by the partners. This helps to keep the costs down, profits up and team suitably engaged at their skill level. How do we compare in our business?

Outsource – Many businesses around the globe are outsourcing jobs, parts of roles and many specifically defined tasks. Bookkeeping, accounting, call centres, legal work, design and drafting and many more. Given language and cultural differences this form of outsourcing operates best when the tasks are clearly defined, and the process is well laid out. Labour rates, penalty rates and the ease of technology all go to make this workable.

Delegate – A good example of this is one of my current clients that insists on spending around two days per month tidying up the accounts for the business. Following through some of the processes above and some staff training the two days have now been delegated and the owner is focusing on continued growth and profitability. Sounds simple, however this was achieved over a six-month period.

Cashflow Sin #11

WOW – this is a BIG one! Set a plan to go through your business to apply the above process to each role and function. Start with your own to give yourself the time and headspace to focus on the remainder. Go hard and remember your time is the most valuable and needs to

Chapter 4

have some free time attached to give you headspace to focus on your business' future!

Dollars & SENSE EXERCISE #11

Smarter business does lead to stronger cashflow. Finding the smartest and most affordable way for things to get done will strengthen your bottom line and ultimately the cash position.

> For free stuff, useful tips and course work, head to our website: www.thecashflowcoach.global

WYSIWYG

What You See Is What You Get: this acronym was developed in the early days of computers. However, I like to apply it to the business world by showing business owners that the output from their team is exactly what the output from the team is. Not wanting to confuse you here but what's getting done is what's getting done. What's not getting done is what's not getting done.

The real question is what's getting done that doesn't need to be getting done and what's not getting done that needs to be getting done. Working off a base assuming nothing needs to be done and only adding in things to be done when everyone agrees that it must be done is a great way of streamlining the structure of your business.

The other side of the coin I see too often is that too many critical things in a business that really need to be done are not getting done. These are often best identified by freeing up the owners or the managers headspace to give them time to focus on and prioritise that amongst their team.

Agility

Flexibility. Adaptability. Being of a mindset of being able to respond and thinking how best to respond. Being focused on what is needed in the business at the time. This is what agile is being about.

I can get really frustrated in some businesses where people are locked in to very well-defined and very narrow roles. They have blinkers on about keeping people in these roles.

Maybe it's a failing on their part, maybe it's a failing on the part of the business owner and leadership group not to have all employees multi-skilled and multi-trained. There are so many times where I see parts of a business working hard and having a lot on the go and then another part of the business is really quiet. It would be great if we could cross-skill so that any increases and decreases in workload could be shared evenly across everybody.

Sometimes this may mean cross-skilling a couple of people so that they can move between different areas in the business as required. This is often the case with people away on holidays; so often, businesses take a person being away to mean that their entire job needs to be done by somebody else. A job is just an accumulation of different tasks and the business may be best served being able to split out the tasks and allocate them across several people, so the job still gets done. It's great to have flexibility, and a flexible mindset within the business really makes running the business a lot easier.

Traction

How do we get traction with this to better understand and act upon our costs in business? We can always dissect the costs in our Profit and Loss, maybe ranking them from highest to lowest to see where we can get the best value from refocusing expenditure. This a great starting point, especially where the business operates in a single product range.

Where the business has multiple income streams then my preference is to group costs by the activity they relate to. This helps better determine the cost activity and profitability of each income stream where it is separable. Most likely your Profit and Loss has all Marketing, Sales and Administration costs grouped in together. What would it tell you about your business if you were to allocate all Marketing costs together, all Sales costs together and all Administration costs together? I guess you might be quite surprised at the breakdown of each group and how easily it is to attach a performance measure to each. Let's pull one of these apart.

Sales costs are likely to have part of the wages and their on-costs account. The Sales team would occupy part of the office lease costs and be using marketing materials like brochures. They would also utilise some of the phone accounts, vehicles, entertainment and the like. We are looking for an educated estimate here, not the last $1 in costs. This gets us closer to where the true investment in sales is each month and we can now better assess the return on this investment.

Chapter 4

Cashflow Sin #12

Ultimately the most agile businesses and business owners are best positioned to take advantage of opportunities moving forward. Giving this focus and attention will build a business better able to change and adapt over time. The fast-paced world we live in better serves those that learn and unlearn faster than their competitors.

Dollars & SENSE EXERCISE #12

Getting traction on this is the responsibility of the business owner, either directly or through others. Be creative but get it done!

When you think you have got to the end of the process it's just the beginning of the next cycle. There is constant pressure on costs and profits. We are part of an ever-changing world. Innovation is imperative to be the best of breed in our industry. Business is a constant and never-ending improvement process.

For free stuff, useful tips and course work, head to our website: www.thecashflowcoach.global

Chapter 5
It's a Balance Sheet for a Reason

Why is it difficult to understand?

Business owners often struggle to understand their Balance Sheet. I struggle to understand some of them myself. I guess some of this is the mystique of the accounting profession. I also think sometimes it is beyond some bookkeepers' skills to properly reconcile and update this and it becomes one of those accounting things that the accountant does each year.

I understand that some of the information will be updated by the accountants when final accounts and tax returns are completed.

It's simple really, for every entry that goes in the accounting system there must be a corresponding other side to the entry. Every transaction will have at least one debit and one credit at a minimum. It amazes me beyond belief that half the business owners that I talk to don't know that a Balance Sheet exists. Of the half that are left, half of them know it exists but have no idea what it is and have never looked at it. Of the remaining business owners, I find very few use the Balance

Sheet to enhance their business or to help with decision making.

It's simple, the Balance Sheet has **Assets** - items of value you own. **Liabilities** are what you owe - that you'll need to pay out over a period. Both are broken down by Current and Noncurrent. Simply put, Current indicates it is cash convertible within the next twelve months or due and payable within the next twelve months. Noncurrent is outside of this time for longer than twelve months.

Balance Sheet

Asset	Liabilities
Current	Current
Non-Current	Non-Current
	Owners Equity

Equity is simply the difference between the two, Assets less Liabilities. If this is positive, then you have Equity (value) in the business. If the Business Equity is negative, then you have negative Equity. So, what is the importance of a Balance Sheet and why is relying solely on a Profit and Loss for decision making so dangerous for your business?

There's a whole heap of financial information that can be determined from a Balance Sheet. It's not the place to go into the details of all the accounting ratios, business valuations, and other great shareholder information that is contained in this report. My goal is to get business owners to understand that the Balance Sheet shows the accumulation of what you own and what you owe. The cash from what you are owed is your immediate life blood. However, what is just as critical is how the items that you owe impact cashflow in a negative way. This needs to be taken into consideration also when determining cashflow.

The accounting system we use of double entry has been around for a couple of thousand years. The double-entry system is not perfect and arguably has many flaws. However, this system has survived for this long and I can't see anything coming in to replace it in our lifetimes. This is what we must work with.

Does the Asset ADD Value?

Going back to the example I mentioned earlier of $1M worth of luxury motor vehicles sitting on the Balance Sheet parked out the front of the business or in family members' driveways. Let's simplify this and assume there are four luxury cars at $250K each giving the $1M. These cars were leased on a five-year finance lease and with a 40% balloon payment after five years. Simply this means that at the end of five years you need to have paid the interest off on the loan plus 60% of the value of the cars. 40% of the cars' purchase price you still owe. You can sell the vehicle to recoup it, you can keep the car and pay out the 40% or trade in the car for the next model.

At the end of five years, each vehicle has approximately $100K to repay. This means for each vehicle the business needs to pay out $150,000 over five years to repay the loan value of the lease or approximately $30,000 per year. Interest (example only) is approximately $10K per year per vehicle. Meaning that from a cashflow perspective, $40K per vehicle is to be paid every year approximately for five years.

The purists amongst us will know that that's not factually correct but a simple exercise that I use to explain to people the big impact on cashflow that these types of transactions have. We are yet to pay any of the costs of driving the vehicle, the imposed Fringe Benefits Tax (FBT), only partial allowance of GST being claimable and the impact of Luxury Car Tax.

You can't easily see these imposts on the business in your Profit and Loss. It is quite difficult to work out how much these are. There's a couple of components to it that I mentioned above. First one is the interest repayments, the second one is the loan repayments, the third one is all the taxes.

Loan repayments sit on the Balance Sheet and in this example, they are a Liability that is repaid every month for five years. There is recognition of this in the Profit and Loss, but it is hidden in the charge of Depreciation or Amortization. This is the writing-off of their liability over the time of the lease.

Depreciation is another word for the same thing, writing off an asset. I'm not wanting to make this too complicated, but simply there's a $40K impact for cashflow each year for each vehicle, so $160K a year or roughly $3K a week.

Unless you understand these transactions and the impact they have on your cashflow, they can lead you down a path of destroying your business with unnecessary expenditure and causing you cashflow strain.

Balance Sheet Dangers

Balance Sheet Dangers

I have heard several business owners say, "It's okay, it's not going to impact on Profit and Loss." They believe the effect of liabilities on the profitability of their businesses will remain the same or only have a small impact. The reality is that whenever you take on a liability that needs to be repaid, it will affect your bank balance. It affects your bank balance in this way. There is every chance it's going to be in your Expenses on your Profit and Loss.

What the Balance Sheet does is very nicely show in a complex way what portion of this liability across the five-year period is split between the next 12 months and the four years

Chapter 5

thereafter including the balloon repayment. As business owners, this information is imperative for us to determine our cashflow.

Things we own generally have value; however, what is shown on the Balance Sheet is what we pay for things. It is not the recoverable value we would receive should we choose to sell it. Alternatively, there may be a point in time where we'll be forced to sell things and find that our recoverable value is actually very low. This is risk in business; we need to purchase items for a business to be able to generate revenue and generate profits. There is an expense line in the Profit and Loss for Depreciation. I guess this is not included in your reports! Depreciation effectively writes off the cost of the Asset over the period you anticipate using it. The challenge here is that most business owners leave the Depreciation adjustment to their Accountant and judge their business's financial performance prior to deducting Depreciation.

There is no such thing as a free lunch, as the saying goes. When you purchase an Asset, you will eventually be required to pay for it. This is not always immediately. When the purchase is for your business and it profitably generates income for the business this is generally a good move. However, when the asset is not producing income it is more a Liability than an Asset. Particularly so when the Asset is not likely to increase in value over time.

Cashflow Sin #13

Loading your Balance Sheet with unnecessary expenditure drains cashflow, either immediately or slowly over time.

Dollars & SENSE EXERCISE #13

Time to have a good hard look at what is on your Balance Sheet. Assets only have value if you are utilising them to benefit your business. There may well be many items there. Liabilities will need to be paid out, get on it!

For free stuff, useful tips and course work, head to our website: www.thecashflowcoach.global

---

It all falls within a few Cycles

Sales Cycle

"I had a record sales month!" exclaimed the business owner rather excitedly. A few days later he's looking at the bank account and wanting to know why there is no money left. The bit in the middle is the way his business cycle goes. Sales first, then most of us are selling on credit terms so the sales invoice sits in Debtors (Accounts Receivable). At some future point we get a cash inflow when the Debtor pays.

It's easy to forget the bit in the middle. Debtors. How well do we sell vs how well do we sell giving credit terms? It is quite difficult to keep good cashflow when your Debtors grow. A simpler strategy is to wherever possible not have Debtors and collect the money on the spot. When you are dealing with cash inflows, get them as soon as you can.

Purchasing Cycle

There's a similar cycle when we purchase things on credit terms. We have an accumulation of Creditors (Accounts Payable). When we do pay these, we have a cash outflow. When a business is run purchasing on credit it gives them extra time to pay their accounts. If the Creditors and the Debtors are offsetting each other, the merry-go-round begins. Simply put, you pay people when other people pay you. It is often the reality of the situation you are in however this form of juggling can be a very difficult way to run a business.

Debtors show on the Balance Sheet as a current Asset. Creditors sit on the Balance Sheet as Current Liability. We know we have future inflows and future outflows that will impact our bank account as a result.

Cash to Cash Cycle (Cash Gap)

Cash Gap Calculation

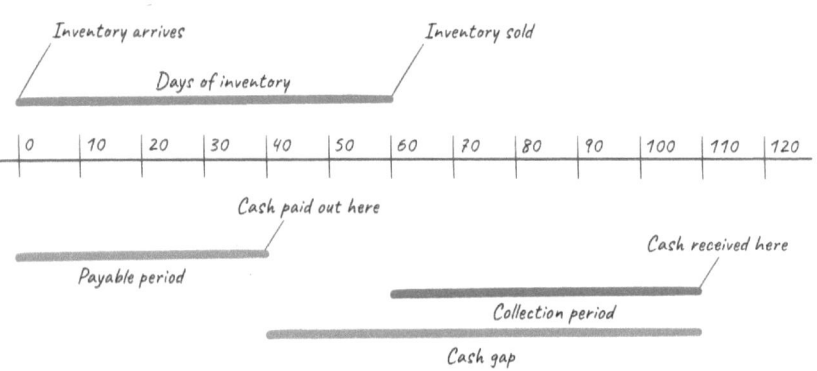

Let's have a quick look at what happens when we join the Purchasing Cycle and the Sales Cycle together. This becomes a driver for our business in measuring our full business Cash to Cash Cycle and what is our Cash Gap, either positive or negative. The Cash Gap starts at the end of the Purchasing Cycle and runs through to the end of the Sales Cycle. The time period between when we pay for goods purchased and when we get paid for the same goods after they are sold.

There are businesses out there that have a negative Cash Gap. This means they can purchase goods, sell them, get paid for the sale ahead of paying for the purchase. This creates a negative Cash Gap and allows the business to use other people's money to fund its operations. Great situation for the business and certainly a goal for us all.

Chapter 5

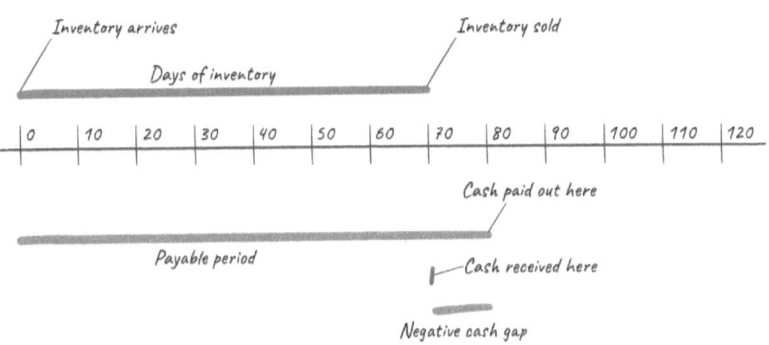

Payroll Cycle and Others

There will be other cash cycles that need to be sorted on the spot. The biggest one here is probably payroll. Employees need to be paid in full and on time. The other aspects to payroll that may not need to be paid at the time are potentially Tax Deducted from the employee's payroll, Superannuation and Employee Entitlements, along with Annual Leave and Sick Leave. It can be frustrating when these amounts are not accrued for in the Liabilities section of the Balance Sheet and there are not the funds in the account to pay these liabilities when they are due. If cashflow is that tight then a good idea is to set up bank accounts for Tax Liabilities,

Smarter Business Stronger Cashflow

Superannuation Liabilities and even Employee Entitlement Liabilities.

Cashflow Sin #14

Leaving your bank account short on being able to pay your accounts on time is stressful. All businesses will have periods of good and not so good cashflow during their life. Understanding your business cashflow cycles is always a great starting point to being on top of your finances.

Dollars & SENSE EXERCISE #14

Know your numbers for your cashflow. Have a weekly cashflow in place, on paper and updated at least weekly. This will flag any upcoming issues and give you time to address them before they become a problem. Remember profit is not cashflow! Get on it!

For free stuff, useful tips and course work, head to our website: www.thecashflowcoach.global

Chapter 5

Head Space

Running a business requires us to maintain a calm, cool and collected disposition. We go into battle each day. We look forward with strategy and backwards into business results. We plan for the future and yet are mindful of the past.

Juggling finances is a distraction. The longer it goes on the more it fills our thoughts, creeping into our headspace. Once in our headspace, it grows like a cancer to occupy more and more of our thoughts. We start to stress about our finances. The more we stress the less we can think clearly and deal with day to day issues. If the financial pressure continues and becomes long term or severe or both, we can enter a phase of 'Financial Paralysis'. This is a point in time when we are unable to get anything done involving finances. Incredibly tough.

Facing the reality of the financial position of the business is always a must.

Cashflow Sin #15

Making cashflow decisions when under pressure or stressed is recipe for making poor choices. Take regular time out from your business to help keep your headspace fresh and open to how best to utilise existing cashflow.

Dollars & SENSE EXERCISE #15

Get your cashflow together and have a good look over it – AWAY from the business!

For free stuff, useful tips and course work, head to our website: www.thecashflowcoach.global

Chapter 6
Stock or not to Stock?

Asset or Liability

I use the words stock and inventory interchangeably in my vocabulary. My frustration with inventory is that it is very easy to fall into traps and maybe not have the knowledge behind how to manage it and how to make sure that you have the right stock in the right place at the right time. That's my four Rs of Inventory Management:
- Right Stock
- Right Place
- Right Time
- Right Amounts

If we looked at inventory the other way and said it's a Liability, how much would you hold on hand? It's not far from the truth if we cannot sell it. Inventory is an asset if it is saleable. However, a motor vehicle is also an asset that will serve you well. Imagine if you had a motor vehicle sitting in the car park of your business that no one ever drove. No one ever used it. All it did was sit there, getting dirty, getting birdshit all over it and needing servicing every few months with no kilometres on the clock. You can see it slowly falling apart. Would you leave it there or would you sell it or trade it in or get rid of it in some way shape or form? Simply put, it would be taking up valuable space in your business that you would want to be able to utilise in some other way shape or form.

When I view inventory through the same lens as an excess motor vehicle sitting in the car park, I see a tremendous opportunity to quickly change the cash position of businesses. I know I've touched on this earlier in the book and it is one of the key components of education of business owners that I think is missing in the marketplace. Simply, that is how to manage inventory. The second part of the question is what are the rules around holding inventory and how do you work out how much of it you need to have in place? Let's start with this aspect first.

Inventory Management needs Management

The first point we need to be very aware of is making sure that our investment in inventory has the right level of security around it. Valuable items are an investment, and since we spent money on it, let's make sure it's physically secure from both internal and external opportunities. As much as you may love your employees, they will steal from you. I know even in businesses that I have owned, I've lost stock because of theft, fire and flood. It is important that inventory is properly insured and secured. If we haven't got these things in place that's a real risk. This type of risk can be mitigated very easily with good insurance policies through an insurance broker.

Chapter 6

Suppliers – Friend or Foe?

The second thing with inventory is to review our purchasing functions. Do we see this as an opportunity to go to multiple suppliers and screw them down on price to somehow get a better deal? Or do we see an opportunity to collaborate with a partner to give them a volume of business to be able to allow them to get their cost structure down and sell to you at a better price and better value proposition?

TUV Pty Ltd

I'm a big fan of working with your suppliers' supply chains to get them to a point where they can take some cost out of their system. Let me give you an example of an organisation I was working with recently.

TUV Pty Ltd purchased a product range in different sizes that accounted for about a $3M spend per year. They incurred roughly $75K a year in overheads by purchasing through different suppliers to try and get a better price every time they purchased the product. Purchasing was constant: two or three times a week. The suppliers had to then organise delivery of the product and get it the factory. Foreign currency movements made the supply price volatile as well.

We began to look at our suppliers differently and asked them to do total supply of the product range for a 12-month period. We gave them indicative volumes of what we would be using for TUV's business. This was a very lucrative deal for the range of suppliers to quote on. When it all came back and we put the numbers together, there was a 7% ($210K) saving per year on the lowest price from what we had previously.

Over and above this, the real win was that the purchasing function was significantly reduced in that role moving forward. This purchasing professional was a great negotiator and locked the contract down. He was then able to manage the purchasing function for this in about 20% of the time required previously. This then enabled the rest of his time to be utilised across the remainder of the product range at getting better deals for the business as it continued to grow. To be able to move forward like this was a massive change for this business but took very simple solution. We may say it's simple however this took time, effort and energy but the benefits were huge.

Cashflow Sin #16

How are we managing our inventory? Are our suppliers friends or foes? When was the last time we had a good hard look at inventory and our investment in it?

Chapter 6

Dollars & SENSE EXERCISE #16

Calculate your true of holding Inventory. Work through your ABC's and check how your stock levels compare to required. How over or under stocked are you and how quickly can you get this under control?

For free stuff, useful tips and course work, head to our website: www.thecashflowcoach.global

Lean

You may remember I have mentioned earlier in this book my love for 'lean'. Eliminating anything in your processes that does not add value, must help reduce your cost structure and speed your business up. Great thinking! Waste costs you money, right? What a game changer for many aspects of your business.

I apply this thinking not only to inventory control but also to all aspects of business. If you're not adding value, you become an unnecessary cost. This is a whole area that requires business owners to really think about how their supply chains are operating and how their business operates as well. What can be done to streamline processes? We want to really look at what parts add value and which parts don't.

Re-Order Points

One of the biggest objections business owners seem to have around reducing stock levels is: what happens if somebody suddenly orders an item and they haven't got it in stock? The concept of Safety Stock simply means having enough stock on hand so somebody orders an item you're probably not going to run out before you can get it re-supplied. This is a matter of having a look at lead times, each of the components you use and how quickly can you get the shelf replenished.

Most of the time, I'm a big advocate for staying at the cutting edge of technology. However, some of the best inventory management systems are manually driven. Things like having a designated reorder-point. Simply put, you keep using or selling an item to the hit a point and there is a reorder trigger. This can be as simple as a piece of paper that says it's time to reorder, or an empty carton to trigger a re-order; these can be remarkably successful.

There's also the use of Kan Ban systems which can be a simple two bin system for reordering that can really help minimise your inventory holding. I've worked with a number of manufacturers where we have been able to implement Kan Ban and it has had a remarkable impact not only on their

Chapter 6

ability to complete products, but also to minimise and hold the correct amounts of raw materials and sub-assemblies on the way through. My role here is just to alert you to the fact that although technology is a wonderful thing for reordering and supply, there are instances where manual systems far outweigh this.

Cashflow Sin #17

Lean is a totally different way to view your business. It may well take some time, detailed work and deep thought to get to the bottom of those functions that do not add value.

Dollars & SENSE EXERCISE #17

How do you capitalise on what you have to get cash in your bank not in someone else's pocket?

For free stuff, useful tips and course work, head to our website: www.thecashflowcoach.global

Stock Takes

1. Financial Stock Takes

I once worked with a business which had about 30 branches around the city and a few interstate. It came to my first month end, and all the branch managers had to do their end of the month stocktake to allow us to correctly measure the COGS for each of the outlets.

The standard practice was that we would have a phone hook-up or meeting on the first of the month to go through any issues. On this occasion, one poor branch manager rocked up to the meeting with her eyes hanging out and looking like crap, not having had any sleep at all. Unfortunately, this was her first stocktake and she had taken things quite literally, counting every single thing in the place including how many sheets of paper were in the photocopier.

In this business all the reorder systems were performed manually. This was the right solution for that style of business. However, the stocktake is done at end of month purely for financial record keeping.

Chapter 6

I had roughly allowed less than an hour per outlet to actually physically count and record information on the stock take sheets. To me, a box is either full, three-quarters full, half full, a quarter full or if it's less than that then I regard it as empty for stock take. We don't need any more sophisticated information than that. So, the lesson here is simply if your stocktake is purely for financial purposes, then a quick and dirty (QAD) stocktake, as I call it, is a great way to go. There is no point spending any amount of time on it. In fact, the faster the better.

2. Stock Take Accuracy

It will work quite differently in your business if you need to maintain an accurate stock-on-hand count to know exactly what you have available to sell or use in manufacturing processes.

One of my biggest pet hates is to see a business that is closed for the day or a couple of days for stocktake. To me this is absurd. Why would you jeopardize your business and lose trade for a couple of days because you need to count what is on the shelf? This comes from a lack of knowledge and a lack of experience from business owners when they believe this is the only way for this to be done.

Quite simply, it is near impossible to do, taking a day to count and get an accurate figure of what it is for your business.

Putting all your resources in the business to achieve this does not give a better result. Let me take you through a much easier way, much more consistent way, and a way that will get significantly better results.

Once you have read and understood the ABC analysis in the paragraph below, you'll get a better understanding.

Your **A class items** are the items that you sell the vast majority of and you absolutely must have an accurate reading. These items are recommend counting every month.

Your **B class items** are less important. However, they still need to be counted and I would suggest counting these every two to three months depending on the volume.

C class items are what you sell very rarely and probably have a very slow movement. I would be counting these probably every six months or twelve months, depending on how accurate your records are and how difficult they are to track. Also, I'm a massive advocate of spending a small amount of time every day counting items on your stocktake, so you don't need to stop at the end of month or the end of year to close your business down because you need to count stock.

Simply work out how many items you need to count every working day, from your As, Bs and Cs. Then do the count and put through any stocktake adjustments that need to be done. Say you have 20 A class items, then you have 240 items to count for the year. Doing this every working day is roughly one a day.

You will be counting the B class items them every four months so. This is three times a year for each item; say you have 70 B class items, then you need to count 210 items across the year. This is roughly one item per working day. It's very easy to find 20 minutes a day.

The hard part is to keep up the right attitude about doing it. This then becomes a KPI for the business to drive stocktakes with consistency to eliminate the effort required of adjusting things when they're wrong or when you run into a problem. I would not recommend under any circumstances, the single focus of doing things all on one day to try and achieve a magic result.

Cashflow Sin #18

Do you need to do stocktakes? Do they need to be accurate? If so, are you using best practice to give better results?

Smarter Business Stronger Cashflow

Dollars & SENSE EXERCISE #18

It is surprising how much 'just in case' purchasing gets done to bolster stocktake levels 'just in case' there is a count or system error. Taking charge will not only save time in purchasing, it will significantly lower overall inventory investment and put money in your bank.

> For free stuff, useful tips and course work, head to our website: www.thecashflowcoach.global

ABC – not only in the Alphabet

ABC - Pareto analysis

	% Business	% Items
A	80%	20%
B	15%	30%
C	5%	50%
	100%	100%

ABC relates to Pareto Analysis. Looking at this theory very simply, it poses that 80% of the volume of transactions will be through 20% of your Stock Keeping Units (SKUs). The next 15% of the volume of transactions generally comes from the next 30% of SKUs. The remaining amount which is about 5% comes from around 50% of the SKUs. The power of this is that we can effectively take control of 80% of our business just by getting 20% of our stock lines under control. What a wonderful thing! If for whatever reason your business gets out of control, we can get it back under control very quickly.

There are diminishing returns from here, however the learnings are clear – A Class items should always be on hand when needed and never run out as they are the priority for the business. B Class have a lesser priority and Cs sit behind Bs.

Where's the benefit for cashflow? The power for cashflow here is keeping these SKU's at a required level so we're not over stocked and we're not running out and our business is ticking away nicely, and these items are not causing us a concern. I've seen businesses where the 50% of most used SKU's are mostly under stocked. The problem here is it you start losing customers you put pressure on your purchasing department because they're chasing their tail trying to keep these restocked. This is the priority for focus moving forward. It is beyond the scope of this book to go into the details on how well this works and how it is calculated. In reality it is not that difficult, and the power of clarification is huge.

Happy Harry

Harry had taken over this business from his father and it was in his blood. A great business with a Global reach. Plenty of upside along with plenty of competition. However, this business had a problem. Customers would send in orders and expect them to be despatched within 48 hours, if not they would send this order to a competitor for supply.

We did the numbers and the business was missing out on 1 in 3 items to supply. Alternately, the business could increase sales by 50% if it could supply all orders within the 48-hour timeframe. Some Kan Ban systems considerably changed the landscape quickly. This process rebalanced stock holdings. Through ABC Analysis the business held higher stock levels of A items and we managed to speed up the replenishment process. Much the same for the B items and not surprisingly letting the C items sell off slowly and only replenish them when needed. Interestingly the C class items were overstocked to the point where overall stock levels remained the same value! We achieved 98% Delivery in Full on Time (DIFOT) and reduced overhead to boot!

Holding Costs

There has been a number of Studies and analysis done on what is the holding cost around inventory. I'm not going to revisit this. I'm just going to point out some of the key items that it takes to hold inventory such as Warehouse space, Insurance, items being damaged, obsolescence, theft, or simply no longer saleable for whatever reason. I'm not keen to measure anything as a percentage of value however it does put it in perspective to say that the cost of holding inventory is somewhere around 20 to 30% per year at a minimum. The more you hold the higher this cost becomes, and it is not easily seen in your profit and loss in its entirety as it is spread a cost across multiple cost lines.

The aim of inventory is to make money from it. Make money through having regular sales to go to a great customer base at a good margin. Remember you bank dollars not percentages. However, the transaction is not completed until the money is in the bank. The faster you get the money back in the bank, the more money you will make out of it. The longer the delay in getting the money in the bank will contribute to the Cash Gap Cycle.

Cashflow Sin #19

I have found many businesses to be out of balance. Well stocked on what they do not sell and running out of what they do. The flurry of activity this creates, and the extra cost can be enormous. Missing business in this way fails to give our business the opportunity to grow and keep our client base satisfied.

Dollars & SENSE EXERCISE #19

Critically assess your business and see how far your business is out of balance. What is the holding cost of this and what is the missed opportunity? Critically assess this in conjunction with the Cash Gap covered earlier.

For free stuff, useful tips and course work, head to our website: www.thecashflowcoach.global

Chapter 7
Look Forward and Know where you are going...

Stuck on the Roundabout

Not sure which way to go? Which way, this way? If only it was easy and we knew where we were going - and more importantly, how to get there. Experience tells me that most business owners are really struggling to have clear direction and a clear pathway to get to where they want to go. The unfortunate part of this is that without having a direction, we often end up in a state of doing very little because we are not sure what to do. This sort of business paralysis happens when we have a desire to do something different, but a knowledge or skill gap that makes it difficult for us to find a pathway to get there.

Follow that one step further, and we find that our financial position can start to deteriorate because we don't have a focus on moving forward. I'm not saying that we need to be growing all the time but moving forward can be doing more of the same and keeping ourselves consistent. When things get a little tough, things can change in an unexpected way.

Knowing which direction you plan to go is motivational! There is something about the psychology of having a target to smash out of the park, something to beat. Having this gets our brain into gear and helps us figure out a way to get there. Don't underestimate this, engaging our brain in this way is incredibly powerful.

Regroup & Refocus

Well done for getting through the last chapter and gaining a better understanding of your Balance Sheet. It can be tough going, and it was probably not the most interesting read for most people. However, understanding this is a key part of being a business owner. There is no avoiding it.

If we look at it quite clinically, it is very possible for a business to have a positive cashflow but be making a loss on its Profit and Loss. Conversely, you can have negative cashflow in a business and be making a profit. Each of these can happen because of changes on your Balance Sheet. For example, if we are spending money on assets we are to own, such as cars, plant and equipment, these will then be a cash outflow from our bank. This could force a seemingly profitable business to have negative cashflow.

Conversely, if we are paying out Liabilities such as Annual Leave, Long-Service Leave, paying down loans or paying off tax debt, this could be giving us a negative cashflow when we believe we are making a profit. The last thing we want is for our business to become a train wreck. If you don't have control over what is happening to the cashflow driven from your Balance Sheet, then it can be a major problem. This is probably the reason why the Australian Taxation Office put more small businesses into liquidation than anyone else. The question always arises as to how can we get a better understanding of this and more control over it, so we don't become another statistic in the ATO's records?

Silly Steve

Here is a classic example I hear all too often: Steve had a good business; he was making steady but small profits and saved some excess cash for an investment in additional plant for his factory. Great decision to purchase the equipment - as it would give additional throughput and a distinct advantage in the market. A nice boost for the top-line sales of the business.

The not-so-good part of this decision was to fund this from operating cashflow. Steve did not have the fundamentals of budgets and planning in place. He had what he thought was excess cashflow in the bank. What he did not allow for was a significant tax bill that would be due just after he paid for the additional plant and equipment. His $350K spend was complete just as the ATO Assessment Notice came through the door. Both amounts were about the same dollar value.

There was no excess cash in the account and what was available essentially belonged to the Tax Office.

Steve struggled after this. Getting his debt on a payment plan with the Tax Office was the easy bit. Making payments in full and on-time for the next year was the hard bit. After a few months, we were able to go to market and finance the pieces of plant and equipment with a loan from a bank. It was not easy, and he was able to fund only a portion of the original purchase price. It squeezed the business cashflow and stressed the owner. Steve was a convert after this and budgeted Profit and Loss, Capital Purchases and Repayments (Balance Sheet) to give a solid cashflow forecast moving forward. It's frustrating that it took this level of stress to get this in place.

Looking Back - Forward

Up until now we have been looking at the outcomes of what your business has achieved to date. It's all about looking backwards. Quite simply, looking backwards does not always help with avoiding the cliff face that could be right in front of us.

It is a bit like driving a car looking in the rear-view mirror. The business world is constantly changing at an ever-increasing rate. Business owners are finding the market to be more dynamic and customers to be more demanding. The rate of change in technology is huge and likely to get faster.

Let's ask ourselves the simple question, does looking backwards help us navigate a pathway forward? I think not. It does give us an indicator of what we may need to change and what our performance level has been in the past. Using our financials to move forward, we may need to change our thinking. While big corporates are pretty good at this, I have found most businesses in the small to medium sector to struggle drastically with these concepts.

XYZ Co

After I graduated from uni with my Commerce Degree, I worked for a $400M turnover business that was owned by two multinationals. One of the corporates that owned shares in the business had been in a fair amount of financial trouble itself. This business had made some bad decisions on a global scale and its bankers at the time were reluctant to refinance it, as the size of the debt was considerable. The banks eventually did finance this business – however, they imposed some very strict financial reporting requirements and timelines.

Let's call this business XYZ Co. It was a requirement to send through, on a weekly basis, a Profit and Loss and Balance Sheet and a Cashflow Statement. The Profit and Loss was by operating entity, not by legal entity. The Balance Sheet was consolidated across the entire business along with cashflow as this was handled out of a corporate office. There was about fifteen pages of information for the business that we were part of.

We were a small, insignificant part of the overall picture for this corporate business. The operating week finished at 7AM on a Monday morning and we were required to have the weekly results through to the Board by Midday Thursday. The interesting thing here was that the reports were required to be done in that time frame without exception, no-excuses - not even for Christmas or Easter.

A key aspect of this financial reporting was the comparisons to Budget and the financial performance in the previous year. We were reporting on a weekly basis and financial budgets for that the year were done on a weekly basis.

We had serious requirements around variances and explaining differences from actual results versus budgeted, making sure the Board were across the reasons for it.

We were required to budget for the changes in the Balance Sheet. This was a significant part of cashflow for this business.

This business was losing a significant amount of money. One of the key ways of turning this business around and getting it to head back into profit was getting a full and detailed Budget

Chapter 7

in place. This way the owners knew the business was moving forward. Simply put, the Budget became an agreement between the owners of the business and the employees of the business as to how the business would perform over the next twelve months and beyond. The discipline of being able to break a year down into 52 weeks and drive that on a financial basis had a significant impact on the speed at which that business was turned around. Ultimately this limited the money it lost and maximised the upside potential as quickly as possible.

Know where you are going

Knowing where you plan to go and measuring your performance against how far you've come becomes a fundamental mindset shift for business owners. How do you know if you're moving forward if you don't know what your benchmarks are?

An operating budget simply tells you how your Profit and Loss looks each week or month moving forward for the next twelve months. The Budget also predicts how your Balance Sheet is going to look twelve months out. Having both an Operating (Profit and Loss) and a Capital Expenditure (Assets) Budget forms the basis of how you anticipate your cashflow will look over the same period. You need both documents to achieve this.

Financials - Actual vs Budget

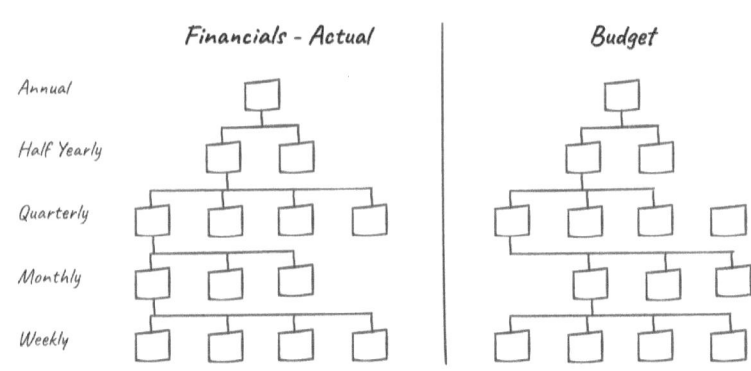

Operating in a way to be Accountable to YOUR Budget

Scaling this back to benefit a small to medium sized business is not as complex or as daunting as it may seem from what I said above. Most corporate entities may want to know weekly Profit and Loss. I think it's important that smaller businesses know their sales on a weekly basis at a minimum. In addition, they have a fair estimate of what their costs are to quickly determine if they are trading profitably on a weekly basis. It may not be as important to run a weekly budget but simply have a monthly one. Certainly monthly, not any longer.

Knowing the key drivers of your business from a cost perspective on a weekly basis is imperative. For example, I've worked with manufacturing businesses where labour is one of the biggest costs. When a business has been in a tight financial situation, we instil the discipline of making sure that the labour costs are measured daily. That has meant accumulating the timesheets and spreadsheeting the actual wages cost each and every day to ensure that the production is at the level we anticipated. This may sound like a complex task, but if we are wanting to cut out the aspects of the business that are not adding value and trying to drive profitability, it becomes an essential aspect of it. Interestingly, whenever we have implemented this across any business, we have been able to tighten costs or achieve more with existing - or both!

To help achieve and exceed budget performance in retail businesses, on a daily or sometimes even part day basis we have measured the number of customers coming through the door, average spend per customer and done a quick breakdown of the product mix. This is to see what drivers can be put in place at the register to increase the average spend or adjust wages costs for the day. We have compared this to the previous year to anticipate actual trade. We have been able to very quickly see trends. Not only does this mean we have been able to limit our exposure to high labour costs and overheads, we have also been able to drive the performance of people at the front counter to drive revenue. This not only helps build our budget for the next year, it also helps our team focus on our current budget as a minimum!

The Need for Speed

Financial Information

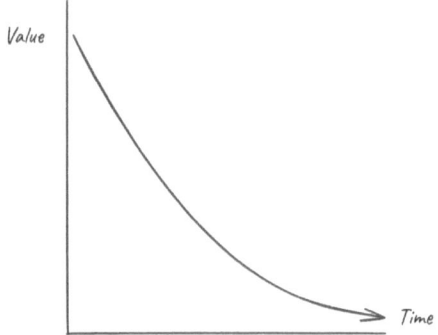

In showing what the cost drivers are and measuring them on very fast turnaround basis, we are able to act. Waiting for the end of the month or for the bookkeepers to get the results out is problematic. It's really important to get on top of this early – it's much easier to drive your business with the revenue and cost drivers that are in place.

It's great if your business has a Business Plan and a Financial Plan with what is Budgeted for, where it's going and how it's going to get there. The reality is that when we start working with businesses, very few of them, if any, have a Business Plan in place that they use on a day to day, week by week basis. Most businesses take time to develop these.

Planning doesn't have to be a full-blown Business Plan and it doesn't have to be intense financial reporting. What does

Chapter 7

have to happen, is that we set our course for the direction in which the business is going and know what the drivers are to get it there. This may seem an onerous task but once we understand what these are, the process is not particularly difficult to manage and can have an immediate payoff.

Cashflow Sin #20

Stay focused and realise budgets are really important to give your business cashflow direction.

Dollars & SENSE EXERCISE #20

Get your Budget together and have a good look over it – AWAY from the business! Expect to have several changes before getting your final version. Clear, peaceful, uninterrupted thinking time will help this immensely!

For free stuff, useful tips and course work, head to our website: www.thecashflowcoach.global

Chapter 8
Cash IS King

It's Up to YOU

Tom's Time was Up

Tom is a great guy. He's very grateful for his learnings, despite finding them the hard way. You see, when I first looked at Tom's business and the accompanying financials, the best advice I could give him was to immediately pull back on his expansion and growth plans and make the core of what he had profitable. Tom was running out of cash fast; and opening four offices at the same time around the country was an immense drain on what was already limited available cash.

Tom is one of the most optimistic guys I have ever met, he has 'glass half full' vigour and enthusiasm. His dream of global domination was to start at the national level, which meant he really had to start in the local market first. Tom had developed a great product in a well-defined niche and a good range of regular customers. However, when I met Tom his Profit & Loss and Balance Sheet were a disaster and his cashflow was non-existent. Tom was on the edge of a cliff and about to fall off headfirst.

It is a bit like wheeling your business into the Emergency Department straight from the ambulance. Keeping this business alive was touch and go. First up it required some serious thought and planning to see if we could move the business forward.

It starts with YOU

Who would have thought when you started your business that you would have to manage a cashflow? When you thought of how good your business was going to be, if one of the things you might need to do to make it great was this? Whether you contemplated the management of cash or not, it is probably one of the most important things that you will do! Yes, it's far from the most exciting thing in the world but this can be one of the biggest stress reducers known to man! It's like a handful of Panadols and a G&T rolled into one.

You will get your cashflow from the information in the Profit and Loss, along with the Balance Sheet Forecast for the time period you are reviewing, adjusted for the timing differences between when you pay for or get paid for business transactions. Sounds super simple, right?

Here are my rough numbers from clients when I first start working with them. Roughly 2% have an up to date cashflow looking forward at least six months. Around 15% have a

Chapter 8

cashflow that is done once a year by their accountant. That leaves about 83% with absolutely nothing. 98% stress about, lose sleep over or don't make business decisions based on cashflow – you can guess which 98% this refers to!

Lack of cashflow is the biggest killer of small business. Why then is it so difficult to convince owners of the need to have a clear view of the cash situation? I'm not here to discuss or educate in mindset and beliefs around money, that subject will be covered in my next book. We are talking about the basics of getting control of your business and making money out of it. Let's look at this the other way.

The number of businesses that fail is huge. Most do so because of lack of cash. If you can see a problem coming, it is far better to deal with this, rectify the situation rather than trying to fix it after the event. Let's look at the biggest killers of cashflow in a business. There is no order to these, you need them all.

Profit

Sure as the sun will rise, not having profit in your business will kill it at some point - and possibly you along with it. It may be a slow process, or it may happen very quickly, however, it is an absolute certainty if you don't start making money, you will run out of cash reserves.

There may be the very odd exception, where you're in a business that is a start-up. It's got long-term growth; however, it's got to have funding to be able to get it through it.

Why don't businesses make money? There will be a lot of unfortunate circumstances where things change very quickly, products become obsolete, businesses don't react in time, or they don't respond to a change in the market. All those sorts of things can contribute to it. At the end of the day, it's going to come back to whether the business is banking enough money to sustain it through lean periods and to move forward into the future. Number one rule of business: never run out of cash. It's very easy to run out of cash if you're not making a profit.

Slow Debtors

Business is broken down into various cycles. Knowing these cycles and how to maximise the benefit from them would help you improve your cashflow. If we are selling on extended

Chapter 8

credit terms and allowing our customers (Debtors) to take extended periods of time to pay us for the goods and services we supply; it is going to strain cash-flow. Having a tight rein, will not only keep the cash coming into our bank account, it also helps to prevent bad debts and potential disputes with Debtors. So now it's time to get to work and measure what your outstanding Debtors are worth. How many days' sales is the debt equivalent to? If you put some effort into reducing your Debtors and getting the money into your bank, what difference would this make to your cashflow?

Business is not Personal and vice versa

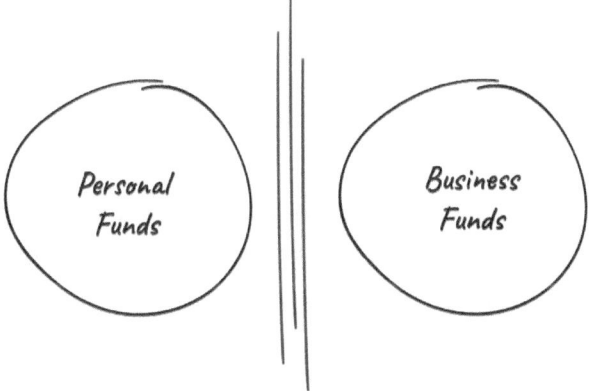

I've seen a significant number of business owners who have drawn a very poor line between business and personal finances. In many situations, they haven't controlled the amount of money they take out of the business or ensured that they paid the appropriate amount of tax. This is often a result of poor record keeping that would not survive a tax audit. If an owner can freely put his hand into the bank account of the business, there is every chance he is going to take more than what he believes he is taking. It may well be his business and ultimately his money, but at the end of the day if this is happening in an uncontrolled fashion, it can put a strain on the business.

Owners would do well to understand that if they have their budget in place and are tracking their performance against budget, then they have agreed how much money they should be taking out of the business on an annual basis. I agree with paying yourself first as a philosophy in business, however you cannot bleed the bank account dry and expect the business to survive.

Cashflow Sin #21

Having clear boundaries between business and personal expenses allows the business to breathe and for the owner to budget their personal expenses accordingly. Not having this in place is prone to failure.

Chapter 8

Dollars & SENSE EXERCISE #21

Get your cashflow together and make sure you have an allocated amount for yourself each week or fortnight. Business expenses you incur need to be paid by the business and personal expenses from your personal drawings. Remember your Tax obligations.

For free stuff, useful tips and course work, head to our website: www.thecashflowcoach.global

Over Stocked and some

The amount of stock that businesses keep ready to sell can be absolute cashflow disaster. Stock is an asset to be sold provided it can be sold and it can be sold quickly. Can it be sold for more than the price you purchased it for?

The concept of a Stock Turn is simply a question of the value of your Stock on Hand (SOH) and how many weeks it would take to sell it all at your current sales level, starting with the total dollar value. You can also do this by Product Grouping or by individual Stock Keeping Unit (SKU). Simply, if your SOH is $1M and your COGS is $100K per month, then you have 10 months SOH.

Hardnosed Johnny

Johnny's business had a certain seasonality and fashion element to the products it was selling. When I was sitting opposite Johnny, across his desk there was an internal window looking out into the warehouse. All I could see were these items and I could see how many times they had written the stocktakes on the product boxes. They had been there for a considerable amount of time; we were talking at least five years plus. Fashion and colour had moved on. We addressed this matter quickly, in the resuscitation of this business, that stock levels needed to be reduced dramatically and immediately.

I received a large amount of resistance from Johnny on this! The stock items that he paid $100 a box for, he was now having to sell for $30 in a bulk buy.

"$30 is better than nothing," I said.

"Yes, but I paid $100."

"Yes, but now they're worth nothing, sitting in your warehouse and they're probably costing you $25 each per year to leave them sitting there. No one will buy them now, unless they are promoted as Special."

The resistance continued as to the impact on the Profit and Loss. This would show the business was making a loss because

Chapter 8

these items were in Stock at $100 a box and would now be selling at $30. I remember saying fantastic! After looking at his Balance Sheet and realising how much tax the business had to pay for previous years, it was going to be a great exercise in reducing its tax debt. In fact, we were going to be able to lodge some amended returns to reduce the current tax liabilities. For a struggling business this was a major win.

Very simply, stock is only worth money if you can sell it quickly. In this business, at that point in time, there was no cash. They had borrowed everything they could, and they struggled to make wages each week. Selling off the items in question assisted in reducing pre-existing tax bills and future tax bills. $30 a box went into the bank account when they were probably lucky to get that. 30% of something is better than 30% of nothing. The boxes equated to $20K. The additional funds paid out an existing credit card that was closed, which saved an additional $5K per year in interest and fees. Not to mention the tax adjustments!

Remember we have spoken about how many weeks of stock we are carrying on hand? Hardnosed Johnny was at 38 weeks when we started work, his business is now at 2 weeks; this is a massive result!

Tax

All business cycles incur tax liabilities:
- The Sales Cycle, where we sell items and are required to collect GST;
- The Purchasing Cycle, where we pay GST for items that we purchase and the net differential between those two is paid to the Tax Office.
- Company Payroll: where we deduct employees' Income Tax from their gross pay and pay them the balance. The difference between Gross and Net is the Tax which must be paid to the Tax Office.
- The final part is Employee Superannuation payments. This is required to be paid into a Super Fund on behalf of employees. I have included this here as the Tax Office has control over recovering unpaid superannuation. Now these items can be lumpy amounts and there are some businesses where it has a higher impact than others.

Let's look at one example, coffee shops. These businesses probably sell 98% of their products as having GST to be paid to the ATO. However, most of their ingredients that they use (like coffee beans, chocolate powders, milk, and raw food items) don't have any GST at the time of purchase. The tax bill for these businesses does not have a huge offset from the purchasing line, just from the top line which gets due and payable. Unless you're very careful on budgeting your cash and keeping some aside, this may be a challenge. The same

Chapter 8

can apply for PAYG and superannuation liabilities, it is going to be very difficult to pay them in full, when they're due, if your business is running at low profitability and your cash management is not tight.

Cash Reserves

There are a couple of different aspects to this one. Up front it's very good internal discipline for every company payroll to establish what needs to be set aside for employee PAYGWH and superannuation. The next step is to transfer those funds out of your main trading account and into a payroll liability Reserve account. The beauty of this is when you need to pay the tax to the Australian government, the money is there ready and waiting. It may be only your best estimate at the time and there maybe adjustments along the way, but it's far better to be approximately right than totally wrong and do nothing.

It's also a pretty simple exercise, at the end of every week or month, to run a report from your accounting system that shows how much GST was collected and paid and what the difference is. Transfer this amount to a separate GST bank account, as a simple Reserve. This can save you a lot of headaches and a lot of heartache moving forward.

The second aspect to Reserve bank accounts, is keeping some business funds in reserve to cover the unexpected. I've been in situations with my own businesses, where they have been forced to close temporarily due to circumstances beyond my control. It's very easy to say these events may be covered by insurance and the like; however, insurance companies are very good at hanging on to their own money and parting with as little as possible to you, in the form of a payout.

Other situations arise where you may hold debts for longer than expected or have an unexpected capital expenditure that was unplanned. I was working in a business once where they kept spares for machinery in the event of breakdowns. Each piece was there to serve as a replacement part, should there be a breakdown. It was regarded as exceptionally rare that all would fail at the one time. There was about a four month turnaround to get these items re-machined and remade.

However, when it did happen, they literally had to hire a plane to send these items off to get repaired and returned quickly, as part of the plant was not able to continue production. They paid a premium to jump to the top of the queue to get this work done and the return plane flight ended up costing about $1M, in addition to the repairs themselves. Yes, in comparison to turnover, a million dollars was not huge. However, due to tight cashflow at the time, $1M was a huge expense.

There will always be situations where cars need new engines, trucks need new motors, plant break downs mean replacing a generator. Unexpected events require immediate funding capability. It is always good to have cash reserves available, at

Chapter 8

any point in time, so you can access them to cover these events. Running by the seat of your pants is rarely a good way to go.

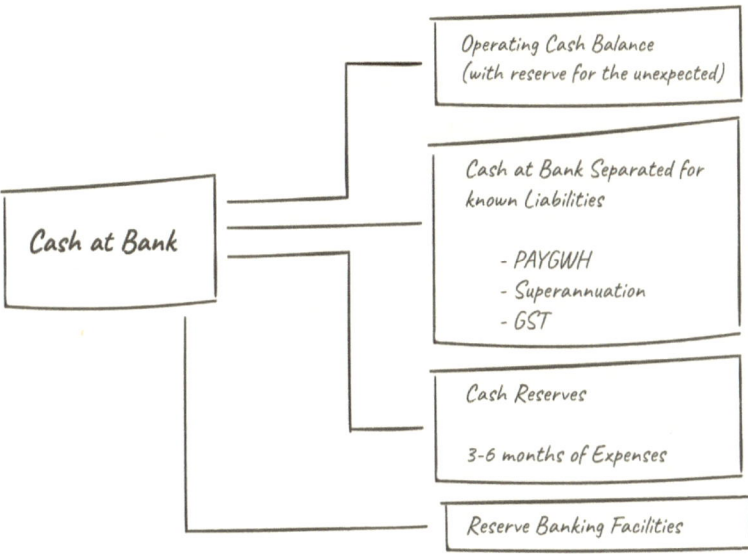

Cashflow Sin #22

Business is not always smooth sailing. Sometimes the wind howls and the seas have a large swell. Having sufficient funds in reserve is mandatory to cover the unexpected emergency.

Dollars & SENSE EXERCISE #22

Have you got your cash reserves in place for the unexpected?

For free stuff, useful tips and course work, head to our website: www.thecashflowcoach.global

Debt and Credit Cards

Business owners sometimes fall in the trap of relying on credit cards to solve short term cashflow requirements. Sounds good at the time but unfortunately short-term becomes longer-term and then longer-term becomes more credit cards to fund the short-term and then suddenly, you've got a stack of cards and high interest rates. More importantly, the business becomes reliant on them. It is an easy trap to fall into because the ability to get a credit card whether in a personal name or a business name, is relatively simple.

One of the other big killers for businesses is the high level of debt that they carry, as they often have been unable to pay down their debt due to poor cashflow. If you can't pay the debt down, you can get stuck at some point in time. Many business owners have their houses listed as security, so if the business fails, the bank can take possession, to pay the debt.

Chapter 8

Not a pleasant situation for anyone, particularly as the sequence goes you may also get behind with the tax office. Either way, the bank moves in or the tax office does, and you move out of your home so they can sell the property to recover the debt.

There's also a big difference between good debt and bad debt. Investing in assets that are going to make money is good debt. Investing or spending money and funding it with debt and having no assets to show for it is bad. Have a little review of your business and establish where your good and bad debt levels are at and how your debts have been funded.

Fraud and Theft

You hear about it in the news when somebody is convicted of fraud or theft. It's a sensational item that catches our imagination and our attention. We seem to think it won't happen to us. Petty theft is hard to stop. Wages fraud is one of the biggest forms of fraud from your own employees. I've had people steal from me many times over in all sorts of different ways. It is fundamental to maintain safe keeping of your business assets – cash, bank accounts, confidential information and especially employees' timekeeping records.

Lack of Owner Focus

When I talk about business owner focus, it is a real thing that happens. Let me put some boundaries around it first. The business is continuing to do what it has always done, and for some reason the owner loses focus. It can be a simple thing that turns into something larger. The longer things are left, the harder they are to deal with, and the difficulty then lies in steering the company back in the right direction.

After a period, running a business can become boring and for a whole host of reasons that is a wonderful thing. A lot of businesses have the same customers, sell the same products, have the same trading terms and similar relationships with their customers. It is hard to keep it fresh and to maintain a connection with your customers and for them to remain connected to you and your business. However, most customers leave a business from perceived indifference, that is, the business owner doesn't care whether they're there or not. Turning up to the same place, in the same environment, doing the same thing allows boredom and frustration to set in and eventually, customers lose interest in your business altogether.

The salient point here is, your business has a beginning, a middle and an end. As the end approaches, it's time for you to reinvigorate yourself or move on. The upside is that it gives you the opportunity to put that business under management, run it remotely, replicate that business, start another one or simply enjoy life until another opportunity presents itself. I think the worst thing you can do is stay in the business, if you no longer enjoy being a part of it.

Monica – One of the Nicest People ever

I remember talking to one prospect who became one of my nicest clients. She was in her business and had been for several years. She had been trying to sell. She hated it. In our initial discussion, she burst into tears, handed me the keys and said take my business as she walked out the door. Clearly, Monica had lost interest in her business and it dragged her down.

To some extent, the nature of the business had worn her down and secondly, it was not really making any money. Monica was essentially doing most of the work and although she had another employee helping her, it was a long haul with some antisocial hours involved. The dream of owning a business had not lived up to Monica's expectations.

We made a deal. Monica had to stay in the business as she would be far better off running it herself than having me involved, trying to run it! I worked with Monica and gave it a two-month trial to see whether we could reinvigorate her enthusiasm for, what was once her baby. And yes, it worked!

We were able to change the key drivers of the business, to get the business on a pathway to making money quickly.

Monica had just switched off and had lost interest in what she wanted. She loved the process. This changed her pathway. She did eventually sell the business though, a few years later, to take a new direction in her life and was very happy with the sale price that she received.

Being Agile

I use the term 'being agile' as referring to the business's ability to be able to respond to factors outside of the business. For example, being able to develop new services and product offerings, or to be able to design products specifically for customer requirements. It may be as simple as being able to have a service level specific for a customer and to generate business from it. Much of the time, this fresh thinking agility comes from the business owner and their headspace.

Having time to think, being able to look at the business with fresh eyes, to examine financial situation of your business and its product offering enables you to see future potential in the market. It's very clear that the world is changing at a very rapid pace. The ability to learn new things and unlearn existing thought patterns, allows you to have an open headspace to be able to see alternatives It is very unlikely that you can achieve this sitting inside the four walls of your business. You

Chapter 8

may need to be outside, in a different place and it may take some training of your brain, to be able to think differently. Many of the breakthroughs I've seen with business owners have come from their ability to see where the business is generating good profit and being able to focus on some expansion around that area.

Chapter 9
Extra Essentials

No book covering smarter ways of doing business to improve cashflow would be complete without covering off some of the basics that many business owners would not have thought of nor sought good advice about. I will keep them brief as some of them are complex and require specialist input.

Taxation

Remember Peter from earlier, how his business turned around after we implemented tighter control of direct labour? Unfortunately for Peter, there is more to this story.

Peter had a big tax debt that accumulated during the time when he did not have good operational control of his business. Peter's Accountant had been liaising with the Tax Office on this and it had gone on for some time. Peter had some investment properties in his name also and the Tax Office came after them and his business. The legal action pushed Peter into closing the business and personal bankruptcy. Peter had not thought through this eventuality and some simple asset protection could have avoided the sale of investment properties and his family home.

CHAPTER 9

The other challenge Peter faced was that the legal entity that he traded with was not tax effective. By this I mean Peter was paying more tax than what he legally could have with better advice at the start of his business. This contributed to the business tax debt over time; however, it would have been very expensive to change over to a more tax effective entity.

The advice here is to get the best advice! Our tax system is very complex and constantly changing. The Income Tax Assessment Act does not even define the word Income – which makes it very difficult!

Knowing the Rules in Your Business

I was working with a client recently that was looking for a new car for their business. There are provisions currently available for immediate asset write-offs below a certain level of expenditure. He rang me really agitated, not fully understanding the rules but expecting the car salesmen to be able to assist. Quite the opposite, the salesmen had no idea of the rules, not even the business managers did.

I was gob-smacked and checked it out myself. These guys are trying to sell new cars knowing a decent proportion of them will be sold to business owners. The tax provisions had been well advertised, even by their own businesses. Why would they not know the rules? We were not asking them to advise on them, just know the rules. Here is a lesson for us all; know the rules of the game.

Business Insolvency

The number of businesses going into administration or being liquidated is huge. When we start our business, we need to be very mindful of this, that there is a very high chance that it could happen to us.

The rules around insolvency are very clear. The roles of the administrator and liquidator are very clear also. Directors of Companies have clear responsibilities around company solvency and insolvent trading also. Ignorance of the law is not an excuse nor a defence. It is probably the furthest thing from your mind when you are starting out; however, be cognizant of your obligations.

Remember how Peter lost his business, home and investment properties to the Tax Office? His wife was able to buy back his plant and equipment from the liquidator at second-hand market value and start again with his same company name, customers and workforce. A harsh lesson to learn however more appropriate business structures were in place and a clean set of financials as the debt had been extinguished. It didn't take long to get back into a new family home and add to his wife's wealth.

CHAPTER 9

Kerry Packer

We all have our views on the fairness or otherwise of our Taxation System. Here is a transcript from Kerry Packer who was at the time Australia's richest man when he fronted the Select Committee on Print Media 4 November 1991:

You made the rules in 1986.

I didn't try to sneak around the back door or sneak underneath this.

These rules were made in 1986, I read the rules, said "What am I allowed to do?" and that's exactly what we have done.

Now why do you want to change the rules again? This is the first, what's happened with this operation going on now, is exactly what those rules were put in place for.

It's the first time it's been used, it's exactly what they were put in place for and we have obeyed them absolutely.

Why do you want to change the rules again?

I mean since I grew up as a boy, I would imagine that through the parliaments of Australia, from the time I was 18/19 years of age to now, there must have been 10,000 new laws have been passed and I don't really think it that much of a better place and I'd like to make a suggestion to you that would be far more useful. If you want to pass a new law, why don't you only do it when you have repealed an old one.

I mean this idea of just passing legislation every time someone blinks is nonsense. Nobody knows it, no one understands it, you have to be a lawyer with books up to here, purely and simply to do the things we use to do and every time you pass a law, you take somebody's privileges away from them.

There is nothing wrong with minimising tax, I don't know anybody who doesn't minimize their tax.

[Panellist: And you were doing so in ways that were contrary to the spirit of the law]

Oh well, I just got through telling you what I thought about that. I am not evading tax in anyway shape or form. Now of course, I am minimizing my tax and if anybody in this country that doesn't minimize their tax, wants their heads read because as a government, I can tell you that you are not spending it that well that we should be donating extra.

CHAPTER 9

We can argue forever about the fairness of our taxation system. No one likes paying tax and no one ever will. I don't think our Tax Office will receive any popularity votes for this reason.

We have our obligations in this regard. What is clear to me is that most business owners have not taken the time to learn the rules of the game.

Taxation can be a significant impost for businesses. We have our obligations to collect and remit GST in the form of Business Activity Statements (BAS). We are required to deduct employee income tax payments as PAYGWH. There are industry specific taxes at both Federal and State Government level such as Stamp Duty and Payroll Tax.

We have specific taxation treatment of entity types such as companies, partnerships and trusts. We have mandated minimum wage levels; worker health and safety obligations; providing for employee retirement through compulsory superannuation payments also falls to the business owner to fulfill.

There are specific rules around selling your business and possible taxation treatment of this. An additional area that is administrated by the tax office is that of personal solvency, bankruptcy and director penalties. Asset protection is a key area for your cashflow should things not go according to plan.

Smarter Business Stronger Cashflow

This conversation around taxation, legal obligations and asset protection is to help open your eyes to the potential minefield you may or may not be aware of. Plan carefully upfront with the right advice and be aware of your obligations!

Cashflow sins directory

Cashflow Sin	Where to find this in your Financials	Description	Chapter
#1	Sales – P&L	Concentration Risk – too many eggs in one basket	2
#2	Sales / Margin – P&L	Price Reviews – do not leave money on the table	2
#3	COGS - P&L	Cost Reviews – paying too much for items sold	2
#4	Hidden in Sales	Reduce or eliminate Discounting	2
#5	Debtors – BS	Get the Debtors in – you are not a bank	2
#6	Hidden in COGS and Pay Reports	Are your chargeable employees billing at 100%	3
#7	Hidden in COGS / Payroll	Monetise the value of Rework and Defects to eliminate	3
#8	Hidden in Labour	Poorly trained employees are a lost opportunity	3
#9	Hidden in Sales	A bit of competition is good for your business and employees	3
#10	P&L	Knowing your daily breakeven helps drive sales daily	4
#11	P&L	Start the process of keeping pressure on working SMARTER	4
#12	Not Shown	The Mental Agility of the Business Owner is paramount for good cashflow and seizing opportunities	4
#13	Balance Sheet	Are the Assets benefiting your business?	5
#14	Cash Flow Statement	Having a Cashflow Forecast is mandatory	5

Smarter Business Stronger Cashflow

#15	Not Shown	Review Cashflow decisions away from your business	5
#16	Balance Sheet and Stock on Hand Reports	Review to see items over or under stocked	6
#17	Not Shown / Overhead cost	Eliminating Waste – "Lean"	6
#18	Not Shown / Overhead costs	Smarter ways for Inventory accuracy and Stocktake	6
#19	P&L / Overhead costs	Reducing Stock on Hand through better balance	6
#20	Budgets	Stay focused to maximise your Budget's potential	7
#21	P&L, BS	Boundaries around personal access to business funds	8
#22	BS	Cash reserves are essential for turbulence	8

Congratulations, you made it to the end of my first book.
I hope with an understanding of the Cashflow Sins and having completed the Dollar and Sense exercises, you've uncovered where your cash has been hiding and how to smash your Cashflow Challenges.

Stay tuned for news about follow-up books! Feel free to suggest or make a recommendation on a subject you would like me to dive deeper on. I can talk Cashflow all day and I love sharing my passion with other SMEs and entrepreneurs. Join the Cashflow Coach Clan.

Too often, small business/entrepreneurship can feel very isolating and our community aims to provide a safe environment to share ideas, offload challenges and as a collective come up with solutions. Find out more by emailing me at admin@thecashflowcoach.global.

If you've not signed up for my newsletters and updates, please do so via my website, www.thecashflowcoach.global, where you can browse the Free Stuff page for further videos, worksheets and blogs. You can also follow me on LinkedIn at www.linkedin.com/company/thecashflowcoach.

Finally, if you would like to discuss your business' cashflow in further detail, please reach out at admin@thecashflowcoach.global.

www.ingramcontent.com/pod-product-compliance
Lightning Source LLC
Chambersburg PA
CBHW032042290426
44110CB00012B/915